A.D.

THE BIBLE CONTINUES

✝ ✝ ✝

THE REVOLUTION THAT CHANGED THE WORLD

DR. DAVID JEREMIAH

NEW YORK TIMES BESTSELLING AUTHOR

NBC

BASED ON THE NBC TELEVISION EVENT

THE CRUCIFIXION WAS ONLY THE BEGINNING.

— THE —
REVOLUTION
THAT CHANGED THE WORLD

A.D.
THE BIBLE CONTINUES

Tyndale House Publishers, Inc.
Carol Stream, Illinois

Library of Congress Cataloging-in-Publication Data

Jeremiah, David, date.
   A.D. The revolution that changed the world / Dr. David Jeremiah.
     pages cm
   Includes bibliographical references.
   ISBN 978-1-4964-0795-5 (hc) — ISBN 978-1-4964-0717-7 (sc)
    1. Bible. New Testament—History of Biblical events.   2. Church history—Primitive and early church, ca. 30-600.   3. Bible. Acts—Criticism, interpretation, etc.   I. A.D. (Television program)   II. Title.
   BS2410.J47 2015
   226.6'06—dc23   2015000682

Printed in the United States of America

21   20   19   18   17   16   15
7   6   5   4   3   2   1

To Thomas Williams

Thank you for lending your creative genius to crafting the narrative sections of the book. Your ability to write stories that help us understand the Scriptures is a gift to many!

CONTENTS

✝ ✝ ✝

BEFORE THERE WAS AN A.D.

✝ ✝ ✝

The Backstory to a
World-Changing Revolution

Today we live in the era of A.D., Latin for *anno Domini*, or "in the year of our Lord." The term was coined in the sixth century when a Scythian monk named Dionysius Exiguus introduced a system for numbering years using the birth of Christ as the beginning point of year one. He labeled the years prior to Christ's birth as B.C., meaning "before Christ." This method of reckoning time caught on and has been used ever since. Thus the birth of Christ is recognized by our calendar as the centerpiece of world history.

The alternate designations for marking time, such as C.E., meaning "common era," and B.C.E., "before the common era," are exactly parallel to A.D. and B.C. Though the terms are different, the numbering system is the same, so the year C.E. 2015 is also the year A.D. 2015. But even if the references to "our Lord" and "Christ" are removed, this doesn't change the fact that the coming of Christ was a watershed event. It rightly stands at the center of our reckoning of time, with the years radiating out from it both backward and forward, receding into the past and advancing into the future. Clearly the coming of Christ is, and always will be, the most meaningful, astounding, and transformational event in the history of planet Earth.

This transformation that Christ brought about was revolutionary in the truest sense of the word. He raised a banner of resistance against the tyranny of evil that had invaded the earth in Eden and called all of humanity to join him in a march toward certain victory. It was a movement that turned the world upside down.

Most people in the Western world know at least the broad brushstrokes of who Jesus was. His birth is celebrated every Christmas, his parables are well known, and some of his sayings are part of our vernacular. But the most revolutionary part of his life is revealed in his crucifixion and resurrection. This was why he came, and this is what sparked the revolution. These events removed the barrier of sin between people and God. After his resurrection, Christ instructed his disciples to spread the news about the salvation he offers throughout all nations.

This book tells the story of his disciples' diligence, dedication, and difficulties in accomplishing this mission to call people to turn their backs on sin and follow Christ. In short, it's the story of the world's greatest resistance movement, the Christian church. It explores the church's founding, its reason for existence, its rocky beginnings, and the deep roots it put down to become what it is today. In other words, these pages will show why the centuries since the birth of Christ are called A.D.—anno Domini—the years when the world was completely revolutionized by the coming of our Lord.

The original story of the beginnings of the church is found in the first eleven chapters of the New Testament book of Acts. (Acts is short for "The Acts of the Apostles.") The book you are now holding retells that story in dramatic form. Every incident is related with great care for biblical accuracy, but the accounts have been expanded to bring to life the drama that was certainly present in the actual events. This retelling includes certain assumptions about what the characters might have done or thought in various situations based on the biblical facts and historical context that illuminate some of the spaces between those facts.

In addition to recounting the church's story, each chapter offers a look at what these historical events mean to us today. The revolution that shaped the church wasn't isolated to the first century; it provides inspiration and information that can benefit us in the here and now.

The B.C. Mind-Set

The events, setting, and attitudes depicted in the book of Acts were shaped by centuries of Jewish beliefs, mind-sets, traditions, tensions, and conflicts. We can best understand the story if we know something of its historical context. These three key points offer a brief overview of Israel's history, providing the background needed to grasp the events portrayed in this book.

A Special Nation with a Special Purpose

The story of the nation of Israel began in the twentieth century B.C., when God called a man named Abraham (initially Abram) and guided him out of Mesopotamia to the land of Palestine, on the eastern edge of the Mediterranean Sea. God promised Abraham that he would make his descendants into a great nation and that through him all the nations of the earth would be blessed (Genesis 12:1-7). As the first step in fulfillment of that promise, Abraham became the founder of the nation of Israel.

This growing nation endured four centuries of slavery in Egypt until the great leader Moses led them to freedom. He gave them a set of laws written by God himself, governing diet, hygiene, relationships, property, and rituals. Then Moses brought the Israelites to the land God had promised to Abraham. Many years later, Israel became a shining star among Middle Eastern nations under the rule of their great king David and his son Solomon. But immediately after King Solomon's death, the nation began a downward slide.

A primary cause of the decline was Solomon's tendency toward excess. He began his reign in humility and wisdom, dedicating himself to building the Temple, which was one of the wonders of the ancient world. But as the nation grew in prosperity, he spent lavishly on palaces, horses, chariots, servants, feasts, and many other extravagances. He kept a harem of one thousand women, mostly to build alliances with other nations, and allowed these women to set up worship centers to their foreign gods.

Decline and Fall

After Solomon died, the nation of Israel split in two when the ten northern tribes rebelled against heavy taxation. These tribes retained the name Israel while the two southern tribes, Judah and Benjamin, took the name of the dominant tribe, Judah. The idol worship brought into the country by Solomon's wives took root and began to plunge both nations into a spiral of decadence and decline. The northern tribes plummeted quickly, and in 722 B.C. they were conquered and deported by the Assyrians. They never again existed as a nation. Judah lasted almost a century and a half longer, but in 586 B.C. the Babylonians conquered and deported them to Babylon, a city located in what is now Iraq.

The Jews reacted to the disastrous fall of their nation by rebounding spiritually. They repented of their sin, and in the humiliation of captivity, they began a serious attempt to obey God's laws. They took comfort in their prophets' predictions that a Messiah would come and deliver them from their enemies and into a glorious age far surpassing that of David and Solomon.

The Prophesied Deliverer

The Jewish Tanakh (which Christians call the Old Testament) contained more than 350 prophecies concerning the promised Messiah. Isaiah, who prophesied during the years of Israel's and

Judah's decline, foresaw many details about this coming deliverer, including his virgin birth, lineage, ministry, rejection, suffering, death, and resurrection.

One recurring prophecy in particular gave the Jews their sense of specialness that so often infuriated those around them. The prophets foretold that this great Messiah would not only liberate and rule Israel, he would also extend Israel's rule over all the world. The prophet Daniel wrote, "During the reigns of those kings, the God of heaven will set up a kingdom that will never be destroyed or conquered. It will crush all these kingdoms into nothingness, and it will stand forever" (Daniel 2:44). Based on this and similar prophecies, the Jews believed that under their coming Messiah, they were destined to rule the entire world.

The Medo-Persians conquered Babylon and allowed the captive Jews to return to their homeland and rebuild Jerusalem. But the time was not yet right for the nation to fulfill its glorious prophetic future or even rise to the glory of its golden age under David and Solomon. The Jewish nation continued to be overrun by one nation after another. They were conquered next by the Greeks in 332 B.C. and then by the Romans in 63 B.C.

WHAT DOES THE TITLE *MESSIAH* MEAN?

Messiah is the English translation of the Hebrew word *mashiach*, which refers to a high priest or king whose reign was initiated by the ceremonial anointing of oil. More simply, it means "the anointed one." The word soon came to mean a deliverer or a savior of a nation or group of people. In the Old Testament, the term is often applied to the coming deliverer of Israel, who would rescue the Jews from bondage and oppression.

The Romans divided the Jewish territory into three provinces: Judea (the Greek name for Judah) to the south, Galilee to the north, and Samaria in between. Galilee was ruled by puppet kings in the line of Herod the Great, and Judea was ruled by a Roman-appointed governor.

This was the state of the Jewish nation in A.D. 33 when the revolution described in this book began. It was the fulfillment of the promise to Abraham and the nation of Israel—the nation God had raised up to bring Jesus the Messiah to the world.

The Messiah was about to turn the known world upside down. Who would be ready?

CHAPTER I

THE DAY GOD DIED

✝ ✝ ✝

How God's Chosen Nation
Murdered Its Own King

Matthew 26–27; Mark 14–15; Luke 22–23; John 18–19

PONTIUS PILATE HAD A DILEMMA ON HIS HANDS. It was the Jewish holy week of Passover, and Jerusalem, a city of about 50,000 people, was packed with some 150,000 celebrants from Middle Eastern and Mediterranean nations. As the Roman governor of Judea, Pilate had good reason for concern. Since the Romans had conquered the fiercely independent nation of Israel in 63 B.C., insurrections were a constant threat as groups of nationalist zealots smarting under Roman occupation frequently rose up to defy their conquerors.

The volatility in the atmosphere was palpable. Such an influx of people was difficult to manage under the best of conditions, but on this particular Passover in A.D. 33, the tension was ratcheted up several notches by rumors that the miracle-working rabbi named Jesus would be present. Many Jews thought this man was the long-awaited Messiah. The last thing Pilate wanted was a report to

Caesar that he had allowed a revolt against Roman authority in this already explosive region. As Roman procurators did at every Jewish feast, Pilate brought hundreds of Roman soldiers into Jerusalem to enforce order.

The elite Jewish ruling council, known as the Sanhedrin, believed in a coming Messiah, and they were on the lookout for him. They thought the one who would release them from their oppressors would be a powerful ruler, a man of religious and political clout. This Jesus did not fit their expectations. He was born in obscurity to poor parents, he had no formal education, he appeared to be nothing more than an itinerant street preacher, and he mixed with the rabble—not only with common fishermen, tradesmen, and turncoat tax collectors, but also with known sinners, such as prostitutes, and ceremonially unclean people, including lepers.

The members of the Sanhedrin were frustrated by Jesus, who seemed to have no respect for the religious leaders' traditions and,

THE PASSOVER

Passover is an annual feast that draws its name from an event that occurred in the thirteenth century B.C. when the Israelites were slaves in Egypt. Moses had warned the stubborn Pharaoh that if he did not set the Israelites free, God would inflict death on every firstborn child in Egypt. To ensure that the Israelites were saved, God instructed them to cover their doorways with lamb's blood. The death angel would then "pass over" every marked house, sparing the firstborn within. On the night of Passover, the firstborn of those living under the blood of the lamb were spared while the Egyptian firstborns perished. In the wake of such loss, Pharaoh finally relented and allowed the Israelites to leave Egypt. For the first time in more than four hundred years, they were a free people.

THE SANHEDRIN

The Sanhedrin was the Jewish ruling council composed of seventy men chosen from the chief priests, scribes (men highly educated in Jewish law), and elders of Judea. The high priest served as the group's leader. The Sanhedrin arbitrated criminal, civil, and religious law. It had its own police force and could inflict punishments such as imprisonment, fines, and scourging. But the Jewish council was forbidden from imposing the death penalty, which was only to be administered by the Roman governor.

in their eyes, no respect for the Law of Moses. They were particularly outraged by his seeming violations of the Sabbath rules. One of the Ten Commandments is "Remember to observe the Sabbath day by keeping it holy" (Exodus 20:8). This meant that no work was to be done on the seventh day of the week. The Jewish leaders had encrusted that simple law with a mountain of restrictions that buried the Sabbath in legalism. Then along came Jesus, flagrantly violating their rules by healing sick people and plucking handfuls of grain for his disciples to eat on that day.

Worst of all, these Jewish leaders saw Jesus as a blasphemer. When he made claims that indicated he saw himself as God, the Jewish leaders needed no more evidence against him. Such apparent contempt and irreverence fit the very definition of blasphemy. The heretic must die.

But there were obstacles. Jesus had become immensely popular with the people. He had won them over with his miracles and healings, along with his vivid teachings, which delivered deeper insights than they had ever heard. The people were flocking to this polarizing figure and slipping out from under the Sanhedrin's control.

It was becoming evident that he was a threat to their power and influence. Popular or not, Jesus had to go.

The Sanhedrin's Murderous Plot

In the tradition of Jewish rabbis, Jesus had surrounded himself with a small group of men who followed him and listened to his teachings. Like the teachers of his day, he was training them to carry on the work he had begun. In the Gospels these men are called *disciples*, a word meaning "follower, student, or adherent." Like others who thought Jesus was the Messiah, these disciples expected him to raise an army and drive the Romans from their land.

Just when the Sanhedrin's anger with Jesus was escalating into a plan to kill him, they had a timely visit from one of Jesus' disciples, Judas Iscariot. As it turned out, it didn't take much for Judas to turn his back on his teacher. "How much will you pay me to betray Jesus to you?" he asked them. They offered thirty silver coins, and he placed Jesus into their hands.

JUDAS ISCARIOT

Judas Iscariot was one of Jesus' twelve closest followers. As the one who delivered Jesus into the hands of his enemies, his name has become synoymous with "betrayer." So why would one of Jesus' closest friends become a traitor? The Gospel of John indicates that Judas was motivated by greed. He was the disciples' treasurer and stole funds from the money bag (John 12:6). Luke 22:3 offers an additional insight about his motivation: "Satan entered into Judas Iscariot." After Jesus was condemned, however, Judas is wracked with guilt and hangs himself (Matthew 27:1-10). The book of Acts adds detail to Matthew's account of Judas's suicide. It tells us that when Judas fell headlong into a field, "his body split open, spilling out all his intestines" (Acts 1:18).

Judas timed his betrayal to occur when Jesus returned from praying in the garden of Gethsemane after celebrating Passover with his disciples. He approached his master and greeted him with a traditional Middle Eastern kiss on both cheeks. This act identified Jesus for the throng of police officers and officials who were lurking in the shadows. As they surged forward to make the arrest, Jesus' companion Peter assumed that the rebellion had begun. He drew his sword and slashed at the arresting official, slicing off his ear (John 18:10).

But to Peter's surprise, Jesus stopped him. "'Put away your sword,' Jesus told him. 'Those who use the sword will die by the sword'" (Matthew 26:52). Jesus picked up the severed ear and, with a miraculous touch, reattached it to the man's head (Luke 22:51).

Peter was shocked. Was there to be no revolt? Just what was Jesus about? Only an hour or so earlier, Peter had vowed to stand by his Master through thick and thin, saying, "Lord, I am ready to go to prison with you, and even to die with you" (Luke 22:33). But Jesus, knowing that Peter had misunderstood the nature of his mission, said, "Peter, let me tell you something. Before the rooster crows tomorrow morning, you will deny three times that you even know me" (Luke 22:34).

At the moment of Jesus' arrest, all but two of his disciples fled for their lives, fulfilling one of many Old Testament prophecies: "Strike down the shepherd, and the sheep will be scattered" (Zechariah 13:7). Peter, however, was not among those who scattered. Though reeling from Jesus' unexpected arrest, he was determined to stick by his beloved master in spite of the danger to his own life. He followed at a distance as the Temple police led Jesus to the home of Caiaphas, the high priest, for a trial.

Peter watched from the courtyard, warming his hands by a fire, when a servant girl recognized him.

"You were one of those with Jesus the Galilean," she said (Matthew 26:69).

Peter emphatically denied it.

But others around the fire recognized him and asked the question twice more. With increasing vehemence, Peter claimed each time that he didn't even know Jesus. Immediately after Peter's third denial, a rooster crowed in the distance. Peter remembered Jesus' prediction that he would slip into disloyalty. Shamed and guilt ridden, Peter fled the scene and went into hiding with the other disciples.

Inside the house of Caiaphas, Jesus faced the first of five trials he was to endure. Caiaphas questioned him harshly, but Jesus offered no response until the high priest said, "Tell us if you are the Messiah, the Son of God." Jesus answered, "You have said it" (Matthew 26:63-64).

That was all Caiaphas needed. In a rage, he ripped his robe and accused Jesus of speaking blasphemy, which according to Jewish law was punishable by death. Caiaphas had Jesus beaten, and then he sent him to the Sanhedrin for an official trial.

This second trial was so riddled with illegal and unjust maneuvers

PETER

Peter and his brother Andrew were the first two people Jesus called to be his disciples (Matthew 4:18). Both men were fishermen on the freshwater Sea of Galilee. They had their own boats and by all indications were reasonably successful. Peter's actual name was Simon, a word meaning "God has heard." Jesus renamed him Peter, which means "rock." This new name indicated the change that this man would make from a fisherman to one of Christianity's first great catalysts. Peter was bold and brave but often impulsive, as we see in his rash act of slashing off the ear of Jesus' arresting officer. Yet he was strong and stalwart in his love for his master. As we will see in future chapters, Peter eventually more than lived up to his new name.

that no one familiar with Jewish customs would think it was legitimate. They tried Jesus at night, which was against the Jewish law. They presumed he was guilty at the outset, which was also against the Jewish law. They hired false witnesses to testify against him—a blatantly illegal act in any courtroom. They mistreated Jesus as a prisoner, scourging and beating him, and they provided him with no legal defense. The entire trial from beginning to end was a travesty of justice.

The Jewish council, having condemned Jesus to death but lacking the legal power to execute him, sent him to Governor Pilate for his third trial. Pilate, no doubt irritated at being bothered so early in the morning with what he considered a Jewish affair, began to question Jesus. He soon realized that the Jewish leaders were seeking his death out of sheer jealousy, and he told them he could find no fault in Jesus. But the Jews insisted that his teaching had stirred up trouble in both Judea and Galilee.

When Pilate discovered that Jesus was a Galilean, he thought he

JOSEPH CAIAPHAS

The high priest of the Jews in A.D. 33 was Joseph Caiaphas. According to Jewish law the office of high priest was hereditary, but the Romans had usurped the right to make the appointment in order to ensure Israel's cooperation with Rome. As high priest, Caiaphas presided over the Sanhedrin and performed ritual religious duties, which included entering the sacred Temple chamber called the Holy of Holies to offer the annual atoning sacrifice for the Jewish people. Caiaphas was more pragmatic than religious. He was willing to employ any means necessary—ethical or not—to accomplish his purposes. This pragmatism led him to scold his council for their vacillation over what to do with Jesus, and he advised them to kill Jesus rather than risk a possible uprising that would bring the wrath of Rome.

would rid himself of the problem by passing him off to Herod, the puppet king over Galilee, who was in Jerusalem for Passover. Jesus faced Herod in his fourth trial. But like Pilate, Herod could find nothing in the man that was worthy of death. So he sent Jesus back to Pilate for his fifth and final trial.

The shrewd Jewish leaders, knowing that Pilate's standing before Caesar was precarious, assembled a crowd of Jews to wait at the steps of the Antonia Fortress, the military garrison where Pilate resided when in Jerusalem. The restless mob presented the thinly veiled threat of an uprising if the governor did not accede to the Sanhedrin's wishes. Pilate, already fearing a Passover riot, felt every ounce of the pressure the Jews were applying.

Yet Pilate resisted. Though he was a jaded politician accustomed to bending justice at will, his conscience was not completely dead. He did not want to condemn this man who clearly did not deserve the death penalty. Adding to his uneasiness was his wife's urging that he spare Jesus, for she'd had a troubling dream indicating that he was innocent. Pilate sought desperately for a middle course that would both save Jesus and appease the unbending Jews.

Pilate had Jesus brutally scourged, thinking such harsh punishment would satisfy the Jews' appetite for blood. When that failed to move them, he tried to release Jesus in accordance with a long-standing Roman custom to free a condemned Jewish prisoner, usually an insurrectionist, as a favor to the Jews during their holy week. But the mob, stirred to a frenzy by the Jewish leaders, would have none of it. They shouted over and over, "Crucify him! Crucify him!" (Luke 23:21).

Pilate now feared a full-fledged riot if he did not concede to their demand. He gave in and handed Jesus over to the Roman soldiers for crucifixion. In a futile attempt to evade responsibility for his cowardly act, he ordered a basin of water and washed his hands before the mob, saying, "I am innocent of this man's blood. The responsibility is yours!" (Matthew 27:24).

PONTIUS PILATE

Pilate was a Roman politician who was appointed governor of Judea by the emperor Tiberius in A.D. 26. He hated the Jews, and they hated him for his inflexibility, brutality, and lack of mercy. In his classic book *The Life of Christ*, James Stalker describes this mutual hatred: "[Pilate] hated the Jews whom he ruled, and, in times of irritation, freely shed their blood. They returned his hatred with cordiality, and accused him of every crime—maladministration, cruelty, and robbery. He visited Jerusalem as seldom as possible; for indeed, to one accustomed to the pleasures of Rome, with its theaters, baths, games, and licentious society, Jerusalem, with its religiousness and ever-smoldering revolt, was a dreary residence."[1] Pilate was in the precarious position of governing a people who weren't his own, and when it came time for Jesus' verdict, he chose his reputation over his conscience.

After seeing Jesus condemned, a deep wave of remorse overwhelmed Judas Iscariot. The bag of silver coins he had coveted now stood as an accusation against him. He could keep them no longer. He took them to the chief priests and confessed his sin, saying, "I have betrayed an innocent man." The officials callously retorted, "What do we care? . . . That's your problem" (Matthew 27:4).

That was the final blow for Judas; he could no longer bear the weight of his guilt. He hurled the blood money across the Temple floor, ran out, and hanged himself.

The King Is Killed

Crucifixion, a Roman invention, was possibly the most brutal, painful, and inhumane mode of execution ever devised. It consisted of nailing the victim through the hands and feet to an upright wooden cross. The pain was excruciating, and there was no way for the person on the cross to find relief. When someone hangs this way with outstretched arms, the lungs are compressed, making it impossible to draw a deep breath. Death usually came by asphyxiation.

While Jesus hung on the cross, the Roman soldiers gambled for his clothing, fulfilling this prophecy from Psalm 22:18: "They divide my garments among themselves and throw dice for my clothing." At this point all of Jesus' disciples had abandoned him except John, who stood beneath the cross comforting Jesus' grieving mother, Mary.

As Jesus gasped for his final breaths, the very earth and sky reflected the outrage of the event—that humankind had murdered the Son of God. Luke describes the scene:

> By this time it was about noon, and darkness fell across
> the whole land until three o'clock. The light from the sun
> was gone. And suddenly, the curtain in the sanctuary of
> the Temple was torn down the middle. Then Jesus shouted,
> "Father, I entrust my spirit into your hands!" And with
> those words he breathed his last.   LUKE 23:44-46

Victims often hung alive on their crosses for days. Jesus, however, succumbed after only six hours, no doubt due to the ordeal he had endured prior to his crucifixion. He had been up all night and forced to walk two or three miles to the sites of his five trials. He had suffered two beatings, one ordered by Caiaphas and the other a scourging with Roman whips. The second beating would have left his back in shreds, causing profuse bleeding and exposing layers of muscle and bone. A circlet of thorny briars had been forced onto his head, causing unrelenting pain, not to mention additional bleeding. He was already so weakened that he couldn't carry the horizontal beam of his cross to the site of his execution, as condemned prisoners were customarily forced to do.

As the day neared its end, the Jewish leaders, assuming Jesus to be alive, asked Pilate to break his leg bones so he would die before sundown. The Sabbath would begin at six o'clock that evening, and it was against Jewish law to leave a dead body unburied on the Sabbath day. Breaking the legs of crucifixion victims made it impossible for them to push themselves upward to take pressure off their lungs, thus hastening the process of suffocation.

Pilate gave the order, and Roman soldiers were assigned to this grim task. But when they approached Jesus, he appeared to be dead already. To be certain, a soldier thrust a spear deep into his side. Blood and water poured from the wound, indicating that the blood serum had already begun to separate into its components—a sure sign that the heart was no longer beating.

With these two acts—leaving Jesus' legs intact and piercing his side—the Roman soldiers unwittingly fulfilled two more prophecies concerning Jesus: "The LORD protects the bones of the righteous; not one of them is broken!" (Psalm 34:20) and "They will look on me whom they have pierced" (Zechariah 12:10).

Among the members of the Sanhedrin was a wealthy man named Joseph, who came from the Judean town of Arimathea. Joseph was a follower of Jesus and had opposed the council's decision to seek his death. He went to Pilate secretly (to hide his action from his colleagues) and requested that he be given charge of Jesus' body.

Joseph, aided by Nicodemus, another member of the Sanhedrin who secretly followed Jesus, took the body, treated it with seventy-five pounds of spices, and wrapped it tightly in several layers of traditional grave cloths. They laid the body on a stone slab in Joseph's newly hewn tomb, thus fulfilling another prophecy: "He was buried like a criminal; he was put in a rich man's grave" (Isaiah 53:9). Then the two men, no doubt aided by friends or hired help, rolled a huge, disk-shaped stone over the opening.

The Night at the Tomb

The members of the Sanhedrin were well aware that Jesus had predicted he would rise again on the third day after his death. To prevent his disciples from stealing the body and claiming he had been resurrected, the leaders requested that Pilate seal the tomb and station Roman soldiers to guard it until three days had passed. Pilate granted their request. The stone that covered the tomb was secured with a Roman seal, and a Roman guard of four to sixteen soldiers was posted to prevent anyone from approaching the tomb.

If the biblical account of Jesus' arrest, trials, and crucifixion ended here, it would be a grim story indeed—in fact, a tragedy like the human race has never seen. But here is what happened next:

> Suddenly there was a great earthquake! For an angel of the
> Lord came down from heaven, rolled aside the stone, and
> sat on it. His face shone like lightning, and his clothing was
> as white as snow. The guards shook with fear when they saw
> him, and they fell into a dead faint.   MATTHEW 28:2-4

The resurrection of Jesus had begun.

✝ ✝ ✝

WHY DID JESUS HAVE TO DIE?

This chapter describes the first of two critical events in the life of Jesus that show why he came to earth. He came first to die, and second to be resurrected to new life. These two events cannot be separated, for one is contingent upon the other. Yet it is important to note just what the death of Jesus did for humankind even before the Resurrection occurred.

We can see the importance God places on Jesus' death by the fact that nearly one-fifth of the Gospel of Luke, one-fourth of Matthew, and about one-third of John and Mark are devoted to his final hours. This is appropriate when we consider that to die was his very purpose in coming to earth. In that sense, he was more important to us in death than in life. To understand why Jesus' death is so important for us, we must go back to the beginning.

It All Started in Eden

The Bible tells us that in the beginning God created man and woman in his image and in perfect relationship with him. But God also gave them freedom to choose whether to live under his best plan for their lives or to live on their own terms. Tragically, when they listened to Satan, who appeared in the form of a serpent, and ate the fruit of the infamous forbidden tree, they chose to reject their creator and become their own masters. Instead of obtaining independence, however, they now lived under the tyranny of Satan.

With this decision came Adam's and Eve's inevitable deaths. God is the source of life, and by rejecting him, the first couple doomed

JEWISH BURIAL CUSTOMS

A tomb such as the one belonging to Joseph of Arimathea was only a temporary place for a body to lie while it went through the natural stages of decomposition. After a year or so, the skeletal remains would be collected and placed in an ossuary, or bone box, for permanent burial, usually within the wall of the tomb. Joseph of Arimathea's role in the burial of Jesus is recounted in all four Gospels, but after that he is never mentioned again. Legend says he carried the gospel to Britain and established the first Christian church there. He appears in Arthurian legends as the keeper of the Holy Grail.

themselves to die. It is a fixed law of the universe that "the person who sins is the one who will die" (Ezekiel 18:20). Our problem is the same as theirs, for we inherited their nature and the result of their sinful choice, and we have lived out the life they passed on to us—a life of pride and rebellion against God.

But God loved this first man and woman, and he was not willing to leave them—or us, their descendants—in the clutches of death. In his wisdom and grace, God promised the condemned couple that he would send a deliverer who would crush the power of sin and Satan and free people from the clutches of death (Genesis 3:15).

This solution came at great cost to God, for it meant that he would provide a ransom to free humankind from Satan. That ransom would be none other than God's own Son, whom we know as Jesus. He would allow himself to be put to death in place of the people he loved. Jesus explicitly confirmed this to his followers when he said that he had come to earth "to give his life as a ransom for many" (Mark 10:45).

In C. S. Lewis's book *The Lion, the Witch and the Wardrobe*, we see this ransom principle portrayed in vivid narrative. The great lion Aslan, the son of the Emperor-beyond-the-Sea, is the Christ figure in these stories. He offers himself to the wicked queen, who has enslaved Narnia, and allows her to execute him in the place of a boy who has condemned himself by eating her deadly confection. In the same way, Jesus, who is the Son of God, came to earth to offer himself as the ransom for our sins, thus freeing us from eternal condemnation.

History says that the Romans crucified Jesus. The prophet Isaiah says that God did it (Isaiah 53:4). Peter accused the Jews of crucifying him (Acts 2:23). But the truth is, *we* crucified him. He died for us.

Ultimately, we are the ones to blame for the crucifixion of Jesus Christ. The Romans and the Jews were merely the instruments that brought about his death. He took the punishment we deserve and carried the awful weight of our guilt to the grave. God picked the best that heaven could offer, his own Son, and sent him here to die in order to pay the penalty for our sins.

The Five Responses to Jesus' Death

In spite of how crucial Jesus' death is, not everyone reacts to it in a positive way. Some people are indifferent, some are antagonistic, and some are grateful. All of these attitudes were reflected by people who witnessed the crucifixion of Jesus—and they are precisely the same attitudes people hold toward Jesus today.

THE RESPECTING MASSES

Luke 23:33, 35 says that when Jesus and his executioners "came to a place called The Skull, they nailed him to the cross. . . . The crowd watched." Masses of people stood by on that day, watching the King of kings die. They were mere onlookers, unaffected and uninvolved. They saw the scene as a mere curiosity. Many of them had no doubt witnessed Jesus preaching and healing; they may have even respected him as a great teacher and miracle worker. But to them, his death was just that of a good man who had, unfortunately, run afoul of the authorities.

Perhaps the vast majority of people today are like the respecting masses. They simply look on without getting involved. They respect Jesus as a great man who put his life on the line, but his death has no effect on them. They see Good Friday as another day on the calendar and never stop to consider its crucial meaning to their lives now and their eternal futures.

THE RELIGIOUS LEADERS

The scribes, Pharisees, and members of the Sanhedrin—the ones the Jews looked to for guidance—mocked Jesus as he died on the cross, saying, "He saved others, let him save himself if he is really God's Messiah" (Luke 23:35). Matthew shows us the full extent of their ridicule by reporting their insulting body language. They were "shaking their heads in mockery. 'Look at you now!' they yelled at him. 'You said you were going to destroy the Temple and rebuild it in three days. Well then, if you are the Son of God, save yourself and come down from the cross!'" (Matthew 27:39-40).

Attempting to mock the Lord with his own words, the religious leaders failed to understand two crucial points. The first was that the temple he was referring to was his own body, not the Temple in Jerusalem. These religious leaders would destroy his body, but it would be raised back to life in three days. Second, they did not understand that Jesus possessed all the power needed to descend from the cross. But it was for their sakes—for all of our sakes—that he harnessed his power. If he had come down and saved himself, the entire population of the world—past, present, and future—would have been condemned eternally.

The chief priests, scribes, Pharisees, and elders, not to mention the entire Sanhedrin, should have been the ones to lead the people to belief in their Messiah. Instead, they mocked the Savior of the world. Sadly, the same thing happens today, too. Some people go out of their way to make fun of Jesus and those who follow him. What they don't realize is that God's silence in the face of mockery is not because he's powerless but rather because he's patient, waiting for the right time for his full glory to be revealed.

THE ROMAN SOLDIERS

These men were trained in the art of brutality, and the argument can be made that the soldiers were just doing their jobs. But they actually went further than that. They paid Jesus no respect. They mocked him mercilessly. They even gambled for his clothes at the foot of the cross. These were hardened men who looked upon the death of Jesus as just another part of their military duty, and for the sake of diversion, they ridiculed what they didn't understand.

Although we live in an era that prides itself on religious tolerance, there are still the "Roman soldiers" of today—those who actively reject Christ and seek to persecute his followers. This may happen in physical ways, but it can also take subtler forms, such as rejection and discrimination.

THE REJECTING THIEF

Three men were crucified that day: Jesus and two thieves. Both thieves were executed for their behavior with just cause. One of them, a depraved man, heaped abuse on Jesus as they all hung dying on their crosses. "So you're the Messiah, are you? Prove it by saving yourself—and us, too, while you're at it!" (Luke 23:39). Though the dark door of death was gaping open, ready to swallow him, the thief refused to repent of his sin or turn to the one who was able to forgive him.

Some people still reject Jesus, even in their last hour. They know that only he can shut the door of death and open the door to eternal life, but they are held back by their own pride.

THE REPENTANT THIEF

The other thief, knowing that he was being crucified next to an innocent man, rebuked his partner for his mockery: "'Don't you fear God even when you have been sentenced to die? We deserve to die for our crimes, but this man hasn't done anything wrong.' Then he said, 'Jesus, remember me when you come into your Kingdom'" (Luke 23:40-42).

The repentant thief serves as a reminder that as long as we still have breath, it is not too late to turn to Christ. Even after living a life of sin, people can see themselves for what they are and turn to Jesus for salvation.

Which Group Are You In?

Consider your own response to Jesus' death. Every person on earth is represented at the cross by one of the groups present at his crucifixion.

That includes you and me. The question you must ask yourself is, "Which group am I in?" Do you mock Jesus as the Jewish leaders, Roman soldiers, and unrepentant thief did? Do you simply disregard him as the respecting masses did? Or do you follow the life-saving lead of the repentant thief?

Our sins are deep stains that can be removed from our souls only by placing them on the cross with Jesus. If you have not relinquished your sins to him, know that this is a matter of life and death. God invites you to ask for forgiveness, accept what Jesus did for you, and let him take your sins to the Cross.

If you are already a Christian, your call is to regularly examine your life in light of the Cross. Turn often to the Cross to see the costly price that was paid for your redemption. As the boy in Narnia was redeemed by Aslan's death, you have been redeemed by Jesus' death. "You were not redeemed with corruptible things, like silver or gold, from your aimless conduct . . . but with the precious blood of Christ" (1 Peter 1:18-19, NKJV). This was the whole point of Jesus' coming to earth. He came to take the death we deserved, thus freeing us from the grip of Satan.

The process of redeeming humankind from death, however, would not be complete until after Jesus was resurrected—an event we will explore in the next chapter.

CHAPTER 2

FROM GRIEF TO GLORY

✝ ✝ ✝

The Murdered King Returns
from the Grave

Matthew 28; Mark 16; Luke 24; John 20–21

MARY MAGDALENE GAZED AT THE GRIM SCENE with a heavy heart. She and her friend, another Mary, watched and wept as two of Jesus' followers, Joseph of Arimathea and Nicodemus, laid their master's wrapped body in Joseph's tomb. The two men then stepped out of the carved-out cave and cut the ropes restraining an enormous, disk-shaped stone weighing almost two tons. Released from its moorings, the massive boulder rolled down a short trough ramp and settled with a thud over the entrance of the tomb.

It was all over. Hopes these women had cherished for three years now lay as heavy and dead as the body behind that stone. Grief and despair flooded their hearts—partly because someone they loved dearly had died, but even more because they had believed him to be the Messiah, the long-prophesied deliverer who would free their land from Roman domination.

But that day, they had watched the object of their hopes die a cruel and tortured death, nailed to a cross by the very Roman Empire they thought he had come to conquer. Now he lay silent in the darkness of a tomb—dead. When the great stone fell into place, covering the entrance of the tomb, the two women turned and trudged toward their homes.

The Mystery of the Missing Body

Mary Magdalene was the best known of the women who followed Jesus, and she had been a dedicated financial supporter of his ministry. No doubt it bothered her that Jesus' burial had been hurried in order to get him into the tomb before sundown, as the Jewish law required. Thinking the anointing task incomplete, she determined to return to finish the job.

On Sunday morning, the day after the Sabbath, Mary Magdalene arose early and walked to the tomb carrying spices to anoint Jesus' body. It was a touching act of love. In spite of her deep disappointment, she was intent on honoring and serving her executed leader, even in his death.

When Mary arrived, something stopped her in her tracks. The dark mouth of the tomb gaped open. The stone was gone—not rolled back up its track, but inexplicably resting on the ground some distance away. Her surprise, however, was not caused by any thought that Jesus had risen. Her faith had died with him. She assumed that the tomb had been raided. Greatly upset, she ran to tell the disciples.

An Astounding Discovery

That Saturday between the Crucifixion and Resurrection was surely the longest day the cowering disciples of Jesus had ever experienced. They had put all their hope in Jesus. They had left everything and followed him with dreams of glory and high position in the new government they thought he'd create after he drove out the Romans and led Israel into its golden age. But now this man they'd invested their lives in for three years was dead. Their hopes and dreams had been annihilated. All they could do was sit around grieving as they had never grieved before.

Then all of a sudden, Mary Magdalene burst in on this gloomy scene and cried, "They have taken the Lord's body out of the tomb, and we don't know where they have put him!" (John 20:2).

The disciples were shocked. What could have happened? Immediately Peter and John jumped up and sprinted to the tomb. They did not believe that Jesus had risen, but they wanted to know what had happened to the body. As they arrived at the tomb, expecting a worst-case scenario, they encountered a scene nothing could have prepared them for.

The cloth that had covered the face of Jesus was folded and set aside, but the linen strips his body had been bound in remained intact, just the way Joseph and Nicodemus had wrapped them. They retained the shape of a body, but there was nothing inside. The

MARY MAGDALENE

The first person to witness the risen Jesus and believe in his resurrection was a woman named Mary Magdalene. Her name is drawn from her hometown, Magdala, located just northwest of the Sea of Galilee. She became a steadfast follower and financial supporter of Jesus after he exorcised seven demons that had possessed her (Mark 16:9; Luke 8:1-3). History has erroneously identified Mary Magdalene as the prostitute who washed Jesus' feet with expensive ointment and dried them with her hair (Luke 7:38), but there is no evidence to support this conjecture. In fact, this scenario is unlikely, because Mary apparently had family wealth and would not have needed to resort to such a lifestyle for survival.

wrappings looked like a vacated insect chrysalis. Jesus had been resurrected right through the cloth; its shape hadn't even been disturbed.

Seeing the grave cloths in such a condition was all it took for John to believe that Jesus had been raised from the dead. We are not told whether Peter also believed in that moment. But there was no denying that both men had seen an incredible phenomenon, and they hurried back to tell the others what they had seen.

Mary Magdalene, however, did not return with Peter and John. She stood just outside the tomb, weeping. After a while, she stooped and looked into the dark opening. At that moment she received her second shock of the morning. Two dazzling angels sat on the stone shelf where Jesus' body had lain. They asked her why she was crying. "Because they have taken away my Lord," she said, "and I don't know where they have put him" (John 20:13).

Then, sensing a presence outside the tomb opening, she turned to see a man standing there. She assumed he was the caretaker and asked where he had taken Jesus' body. But the moment he uttered her name, she recognized his voice—he was the risen Jesus! Brimming

THE RESURRECTION BODY OF JESUS

There was something unique about Jesus' resurrection body. It could penetrate solid matter—not only grave cloths, but also stone walls and locked doors. Many people have assumed this meant his body was ghostly—less solid than physical matter. But this was not the case. Jesus' resurrected body was now fit to inhabit heaven, the ultimate reality, which made it even more solid than the matter in our dimension. Physical barriers like walls, grave cloths, and stones could not prevent him from passing through. This gives us insight about why the stone was rolled away: it was not to let Jesus out; it was to let us in. It was a message from God so his followers would know that the tomb was empty.

with joy, she ran to tell the disciples that she had seen the risen Jesus and to deliver his message.

Word of these mysterious happenings quickly spread among the disciples and thrust them into turmoil. What should they believe? John seemed to think that Jesus had been resurrected. Mary Magdalene was certain of it. Peter may still have doubted. The feelings of the others likely ran the gamut from disbelief to hope.

Later that same evening the disciples were eating dinner, still behind locked doors. Suddenly a man appeared before them in the room and said, "Peace be with you" (John 20:19). The disciples were terrified. He had not come through the door, for it was still locked. Was it a ghost? But then the man exposed to them his nail-scarred hands and feet. It was Jesus! He had indeed risen.

The room erupted with wild joy. Jesus asked for food, and they shared with him their supper of broiled fish, which he ate, proving he was not a ghost. He was alive, with a body composed of organs and limbs.

One disciple, Thomas, was not with the others when Jesus appeared. When he returned, the other disciples told him what had happened. He did not buy it for one moment, saying, "I won't believe it unless I see the nail wounds in his hands, put my fingers into them, and place my hand into the wound in his side" (John 20:25).

Eight days later, Jesus again appeared to the disciples, and this time Thomas was with them. Jesus approached Thomas and said, "Put your finger here, and look at my hands. Put your hand into the wound in my side. Don't be faithless any longer. Believe!" Thomas's doubts vanished. In joyful astonishment he cried, "My Lord and my God!" (John 20:27-28).

The Plight of the Roman Guards

The closest witnesses to the Resurrection itself were, strangely enough, Jesus' enemies, the Roman soldiers who stood guard at the tomb. Early on Sunday morning, they saw the most spectacular sight any human being has ever witnessed. But for them, this event that changed the world was far from a pleasant experience. It began with a sudden earthquake that shook the ground so violently none of them could remain standing. Then a great angel, brilliant as lightning and clothed in dazzling white, descended from the heavens and flung the enormous stone from the entrance of the tomb as if it were a pebble. The unprecedented phenomenon overloaded the senses of these hardened soldiers, and they fell to the ground in a dead faint.

When they awoke and peered into the gaping maw of the now-empty tomb, they knew they were in serious trouble. They had failed at their one critical assignment. And they must have known that their superiors would find their explanation utterly outlandish.

But there was no way out; the soldiers had to report what had happened. Fearing their own commanders, they went first to the Jewish chief priests and explained what they had seen. These Jews knew that if the soldiers' story got out, all their manipulating to get

THOMAS

Thomas, one of Jesus' twelve apostles, often gets unfairly maligned. Throughout history he has been called "Doubting Thomas," characterized as one who lacked faith because, without evidence, he refused to believe that Jesus had risen. In reality, however, Thomas's faith was quite strong. Once when Jesus could not be dissuaded from going to a town near Jerusalem where the Jewish leaders were seeking his life, Thomas urged the others, "Let's go, too—and die with Jesus" (John 11:16). Thomas was a man who demanded facts, and this facet of his personality emerged when he heard that Jesus was alive. He would not be taken in by wild rumors; his faith needed evidence, which Jesus willingly supplied.

Jesus out of the way would be to no avail. Yet they knew that people would ask the soldiers about what had happened that night. So the priests offered the soldiers a sizable sum of money if they would say, "Jesus' disciples came during the night while we were sleeping, and they stole his body" (Matthew 28:13).

No doubt the soldiers balked at this solution. For a Roman soldier—a member of the most rigorously trained army in the world—falling asleep on duty was a crime punishable by death. But they accepted the bribe and passed on the story, with the assurance that if the news reached Pilate's ears, the priests would appease him. These Jews knew, of course, that Pilate was every bit as interested as they were in suppressing any rumors of a resurrection.

The Man on the Seashore

The Sanhedrin knew that as long as the body of Jesus was missing, rumors that he had risen would spread like an epidemic. If only they could find and display the body, the threat Jesus posed would be squelched once and for all. In spite of the unexplained phenomena of the moved stone, the broken seal, the empty tomb, and the many prophecies that were fulfilled in the Resurrection, they believed that somehow this cowering group of nobodies who followed Jesus had managed to get past the guards, open the tomb, and steal their master's body. If they could find those disciples, they figured they could, through torture, bribery, or some other ruthless means, persuade them to produce the body.

The disciples knew the Jewish leaders were hunting them. The Gospel of John tells us that they had assembled together somewhere in Jerusalem "because they were afraid of the Jewish leaders" (John 20:19). No doubt rumors of the Resurrection would lead the authorities to intensify their search. The disciples left Jerusalem and headed north to their homes near the Sea of Galilee.

Now lacking clear direction for their futures, Peter and his fellow fishermen resumed their trade. They launched their boat into the sea and fished all night, but they caught nothing. Shortly after dawn, they gave up and headed toward shore. They weren't far from land when they saw a man standing on the beach. He called out and asked if they had caught anything. No, they admitted sourly, they had not.

The man then said, "Throw out your net on the right-hand side of the boat, and you'll get some!" (John 21:6).

Just who does this man think he is? Peter must have thought. *We're professional fishermen; we know what we're doing. Why is this vagabond telling us how to run our business?*

But since they already had their gear at the ready, they had nothing to lose. They cast out their nets to the right of the boat. The net immediately sagged with so many fish that it neared the breaking point—they couldn't even draw it into the boat. Instead, they were forced to drag it behind as they rowed toward the shore.

"It's the Lord!" John cried as they approached. Without hesitation, Peter plunged into the sea and swam ashore, unable to wait for the overloaded boat. When the other disciples arrived, they cooked a hearty breakfast of fish and reveled in the presence of their Lord.

After eating a breakfast of the best fish they had ever tasted, they sat around the campfire basking in Jesus' company. Then out of the blue, Jesus turned to Peter and asked, "Do you love me more than these?"

Peter replied, "Yes, Lord, you know that I love you."

"Feed my lambs," Jesus replied.

This seemingly odd response was a reference to the prophecy from Zechariah that Jesus had quoted during his last supper with his disciples: "Tonight all of you will desert me. For the Scriptures say, 'God will strike the Shepherd, and the sheep of the flock will be scattered'" (Matthew 26:31).

Indeed, the sheep had scattered, just as the prophet had predicted. Every disciple had abandoned him except John. Jesus was indicating that Peter's responsibility would soon involve the care of that scattered flock.

A moment later, Jesus asked the question again: "Simon, son of John, do you love me?"

Again Peter answered, "Yes, Lord. . . . you know I love you."

And again Jesus responded, "Take care of my sheep."

Then, to Peter's consternation, Jesus asked yet a third time, "Simon, son of John, do you love me?"

We can hear the frustration in Peter's voice as he replied, "Lord, you know everything. You know that I love you."

A third time Jesus charged Peter, "Feed my sheep." But this time he added a prophecy that told this shattered disciple that he would henceforth be a defender of his risen Lord, serving him even to the point of imprisonment and death (John 21:15-19).

To us that does not seem like a prediction to be happy about. But to a man who had denied the one he loved most in the world, it meant complete restoration of his standing before the Lord and his fellow disciples. In spite of his previous failure, Peter had still been entrusted with great responsibilities. This pebble of a man would grow into the rock Jesus had predicted he would become.

This unusual exchange between Jesus and Peter is important because it serves as a turning point for Peter, who, as we will see in the next few chapters, became the most visible and active apostle among those who had walked with Jesus during his three years of ministry on earth.

The Puzzling Promise

Jesus instructed his disciples to remain in Jerusalem, where they were to wait until God the Father filled them "with power from heaven" (Luke 24:49). The only hint Jesus gave as to what this power would be was that in just a few days the disciples would "be baptized with the Holy Spirit" (Acts 1:5). But this concept was fuzzy to the disciples. Puzzling over what it meant, they asked, "Lord, has the time come for you to free Israel and restore our kingdom?" (Acts 1:6).

Jesus' miraculous resurrection revived their hopes for a rebellion against Rome. Certainly he was Israel's Messiah, and now he was invincible. Even the daunting power of the Roman army could not stand against a man who had died and been raised to life. Surely warriors eager for battle would flock to him in droves.

These men remained clueless about the real mission of Jesus. But he did not correct them. Very soon the meaning of it all would fall into place, and as he told them, they would be his witnesses "in Jerusalem, throughout Judea, in Samaria, and to the ends of the earth" (Acts 1:8).

Jesus remained on earth for a while longer and appeared to many— once to more than five hundred people at one time—thus confirming his resurrection (1 Corinthians 15:6). Most of those witnesses were still alive and testifying to the Resurrection two or three decades later.

Then, after forty days, Jesus led his disciples out of Jerusalem to Bethany, where he lifted his hands and blessed them. And then something remarkable happened:

> He was taken up into a cloud while they were watching,
> and they could no longer see him. As they strained to see
> him rising into heaven, two white-robed men suddenly
> stood among them. "Men of Galilee," they said, "why
> are you standing here staring into heaven? Jesus has been
> taken from you into heaven, but someday he will return
> from heaven in the same way you saw him go!"
>
> ACTS 1:9-11

Though these disciples had no idea what was about to happen, the promise of coming power filled them with overflowing joy and anticipation. They stayed in Jerusalem, banding together in the upper room of a residence and gathering in the Temple to praise God for what they had seen.

✢ ✢ ✢

THE REALITY OF THE RESURRECTION

Months before dying, in the last book he would ever write, the famous astronomer Carl Sagan expressed his doubts about the reality of life after death: "I would love to believe that when I die I will live again, that some thinking, feeling, remembering part of me will continue. But as much as I want to believe that . . . I know of nothing to suggest that it is more than wishful thinking."[1] In Job 14:14, another man expressed a similar uncertainty when he asked the question: "Can the dead live again?"

This age-old question is the most crucial of any generation, and it casts a haunting shadow over those who reject the resurrection of Christ. In Hebrews 2:15 we read about those who "have lived their lives as slaves to the fear of dying." The English skeptic and philosopher Thomas Hobbes is reported to have exclaimed, "If I had the whole world, I would give it to live one [more] day. . . . I am about to take a leap into the dark." Without some assurance of life after death, death is a terrifying proposition.

The resurrection of Jesus Christ settles the question about life after death once and for all. This event takes Christianity out of the realm of philosophy and turns it into a fact of history. It proves that there is life beyond death.

To deny the Resurrection is to remove the keystone from the arch of the Christian faith. Without it, Christianity is a waste of time. John Stott explains, "Christianity is in its very essence a resurrection religion. The concept of resurrection lies at its heart. If you remove it, Christianity is destroyed."[2]

It is possible to be a Christian and not *understand* the Resurrection.

However, it is not possible to be a Christian and *deny* the Resurrection, because without the Resurrection, Christianity collapses. If all we have is the death and burial of Jesus, we have nothing more than the martyrdom of another good man. The Resurrection authenticates the promise of eternal life.

Some critics over the centuries have thought Christianity to be a joke. Finding the idea of resurrection from the dead laughable, they have tried to destroy its credibility in the hope of crushing the faith. All have failed.

Frank Morison was a journalist whose life goal was to destroy the Resurrection story. His research into the biblical and historical records of the Resurrection turned him 180 degrees, because he found the Resurrection to be one of the best-attested facts in all of history. He followed the evidence and became a Christian.[3]

As we reflect on the Resurrection of Jesus, let's consider three lines of evidence.

The Evidence from Predictions

One of the most amazing yet neglected facts of the Resurrection is how many times Jesus himself predicted it (Matthew 16:21; 17:9, 22-23; 20:18-19; 26:32; John 2:19, 21). The fact that he foretold it and then accomplished it sets it apart as the most bona fide miracle of all time. A man who goes around preaching his own death and resurrection is either a fool or is God. And the credible fact of the Resurrection leaves no doubt as to which Jesus was.

The Evidence from the Past

Perhaps the strongest historical evidence of the Resurrection is the multiple appearances of the risen Christ. Scripture records a dozen such appearances to both men and women, groups and individuals. These appearances happened in various locations and to various people—in a house and on a street, to disciples who were sad and to those who were happy, on momentary occasions and in spans that stretched over a period of time, in different locations and at different times of day. The abundance and variety of his appearances are among the reasons scholars consider the Resurrection to be so well confirmed.

The post-Resurrection appearances of Jesus are easy to document. He appeared to Mary Magdalene by the tomb and to other women returning from the tomb. He appeared to Peter later that same day and to two disciples on the road to Emmaus. Twice he appeared to the apostles inside a locked room, once when Thomas was absent and later when he was present. He appeared to seven disciples by the Sea of Galilee, to five hundred believers on a Galilean mountain, and again to the eleven apostles. He also appeared to James and would later appear to Saul on the road to Damascus, to John on the Isle of Patmos, and again to Saul (now named Paul) in the Temple.

His appearances were documented by people who saw him, heard him, touched him, and watched him eat. Jesus wanted to make certain that his resurrection was proven beyond all doubt (Acts 1:3).

Could all these witnesses have conspired to lie about the Resurrection? The answer is no, for two reasons. First, there were too many witnesses for collusion to have occurred. Second, these witnesses were willing to die for the truth of the Resurrection, which people would never do if they thought it a lie or a figment of the imagination.

Think of the absurdity of this little band of cowards, having run away and hidden in Jesus' time of need, suddenly being transformed into a courageous band of evangelists who turned the world upside down! Each of them except John went to a martyr's death for the cause of Christ. No thinking person would believe that an entire group of intelligent people would die for what they knew to be a lie. It takes more faith to believe the apostles made up the Resurrection story than it does to believe the biblical account!

Charles Colson, who once served as special counsel to President Richard Nixon, wrote, "My personal experiences in the Watergate scandal convinces me of the historic proof of the resurrection." He goes on to explain that President Nixon's closest advisers conspired to keep the illegal break-in secret. The conspiracy unraveled three weeks later, however, when Nixon's legal counsel John Dean, fearing a prison sentence, went to the prosecutors and offered to testify in exchange for immunity "to save his own skin." Other conspirators followed suit, bringing down the Nixon presidency. Colson continues:

> Think of it: the most powerful men around the president of the United States could not keep a lie for three weeks. And you'd have me believe that the twelve apostles—powerless, persecuted, exiled, many martyred, their leader Peter crucified upside down—these common men, gave their lives for a lie, without ever breathing a word to the contrary? Impossible. . . . People will die for something they believe to be true; but men will never die for something they know to be false.[4]

Clearly, these first-century witnesses had not lied.

The Evidence in the Present
Not all the evidence of Christ's resurrection is found in the past. At least five pieces of evidence in our world today also testify to its historicity.[5]

1. THE CHRISTIAN FAITH
The resurrection of Jesus is the linchpin of the Christian faith. This doctrine that Jesus rose from the dead is what turned the world upside down and separated Christianity from Judaism and the pagan religions of the Mediterranean world. If he had not been raised, there would be no Christian faith. If the Resurrection were not true,

neither would there be anything vital or unique about the gospel. It has been said that if the resurrection of Jesus Christ is not a historic fact, then it is our duty to dig a new grave and bury not a man, but the entire Christian religion.

2. THE CHRISTIAN CHURCH

If the Crucifixion had marked the end of the disciples' experience of Christ, how could the Christian church have come into being? The church is founded on Jesus as Messiah, and a dead Messiah is no Messiah at all. A resurrected Messiah is required to fulfill the prophecies made about him as the Son of God. The church survives and flourishes only because Jesus broke out of the tomb, demonstrating that there is life after death.

Josh McDowell and Sean McDowell ask,

> Do you believe for a moment that the early church could have survived for a week in its hostile surroundings if Jesus Christ had not been raised from the dead? The resurrection of the one on whom the church was founded was preached within a few minutes' walk to Joseph's tomb. As a result of the first sermon, in which Peter asserted that Christ had risen, 3,000 people believed (see Acts 2:41). Shortly thereafter, 5,000 more believed. Could all these converts have been made if Jesus had not been raised from the dead?[6]

Theologian Daniel Fuller writes that "to try to explain [the church] without reference to the resurrection is as hopeless as trying to explain Roman history without reference to Julius Caesar."[7]

3. THE CHRISTIAN SUNDAY

The fact that we attend church on Sunday is evidence for the Resurrection. The original Jewish day of worship was Saturday, but

Christians began meeting on Sunday because that was the day Jesus was resurrected. Remember, the early church was made up predominantly of Jewish Christians. For them to change the day of worship from the Sabbath signified that something earth-shattering had occurred. Josh McDowell and Sean McDowell write,

> The early Christians were devout Jews who were fanatical in their observance of the Sabbath. The Jews feared breaking the Sabbath, believing they would incur the wrath of God if they violated the strict laws concerning its observance. Yet something happened that caused these Jewish men and women to turn their backs on all their years of religious training and tradition.
>
> They changed their day of worship to Sunday in honor of the anniversary of the resurrection of Jesus Christ. Can you think of any other historical event that is celebrated 52 times a year? The most rational explanation for this phenomenon is that Jesus appeared personally to people after his resurrection, convincing them of the truth of it.[8]

4. THE CHRISTIAN ORDINANCES

According to the New Testament, the local New Testament church is instructed to celebrate two ordinances: baptism and the Lord's Supper. The ordinance of baptism offers a beautiful picture of the Resurrection. Going down into the water is a symbol not merely of having our sins washed away but also of being buried with Jesus and coming up a new person, raised to life just as Christ was raised from the dead.

The Lord's Supper is a remembrance of death, but Acts 2 says that we are to participate with joy because it also foretells the resurrection of Jesus. Without the Resurrection, there can be no joy.

Dr. J. P. Moreland explains why Communion is an evidence of the Resurrection:

> What's odd is that these early followers of Jesus didn't get together to celebrate his teachings or how wonderful he was. They came together regularly to have a celebration meal for one reason: to remember that Jesus had been publicly slaughtered in a grotesque and humiliating way. Think about this in modern terms. If a group of people loved John F. Kennedy, they might meet regularly to remember his confrontation with Russia, his promotion of civil rights, and his charismatic personality. But they're not going to celebrate the fact that Lee Harvey Oswald murdered him![9]

5. THE CHANGED LIVES

Before the Resurrection, Jesus' disciples were marked by cowardice, doubt, and fear. When Jesus was arrested, "all the disciples deserted him and fled" (Matthew 26:56). Peter denied three times that he even knew Jesus. After the Crucifixion, the disciples hid themselves in an upper room behind locked doors. Thomas even declared, "I won't believe it unless I see the nail wounds in his hands, put my fingers into them, and place my hand into the wound in his side" (John 20:25).

But once they were convinced that Jesus was alive, these cowardly disciples were transformed into courageous messengers for Christ. They traveled the world, turning it upside down, and all except John were martyred for their faith. Would they have been willing to give their lives for Christ if they had believed the Resurrection was a fraud?

The Crucial Significance of the Resurrection

As we noted in chapter 1, the death of Jesus is of critical importance to us because it was by his death that he redeemed us from the captivity of Satan. But without the Resurrection, his death would have been in vain. The Resurrection completes what the Crucifixion began.

To understand the connection between the two events, think of death as a permanent prison from which there was no escape. This, in fact, is exactly what death was. When the first man and woman sinned against God, all human life was forfeited to Satan, who is determined to see us join him in the misery of hell. But Jesus, having no sin himself, volunteered to take on the sins of humankind as if they were his own and die the death of a sinner. He entered the prison of death in our place.

But death could not hold the Son of God. The Resurrection shows that the iron gates of death's prison have been shattered. Jesus burst through them, reentered his human body, and showed himself alive to many witnesses, proving that death no longer has a hold on our fallen race. It has been defeated.

The good news is that by attaching our lives to Jesus, we will be resurrected, just as he was. If we accept him as the ruler of our lives, we can be raised to the new and perfect life God intended for all creation at the beginning. The Resurrection gives us our only hope of eternal life—a claim no other religion in the world has the evidence to prove.

The body of Moses lies in a grave somewhere. The body of Mohammed lies in a tomb. The remains of Lenin lie in a glass-covered casket in Moscow. On his casket are these words: "He was the greatest leader of all peoples, of all countries, of all times. He was the lord of the new humanity. He was the savior of the world." But on January 21, 1924, he took his last breath, and no one has heard from him since. He's dead, like every other human being who has ever existed. If Lenin is indeed the savior of the world, then there is no hope. Of all the great religions in the world, only Christianity is based on the resurrection of its leader. Jesus Christ alone conquered death, and as a result, he can offer us eternal life.

You can begin to live this new life the moment you give yourself over to Christ. You bury your old life by participating in his death and claim a new life by participating in his resurrection. As the apostle Paul explains, "We died and were buried with Christ by baptism. And just as Christ was raised from the dead by the glorious power of the Father, now we also may live new lives" (Romans 6:4). This resurrection life can begin right here and now. It is a free gift, available to anyone who wants it.

CHAPTER 3

WIND AND FIRE

✛ ✛ ✛

The Spectacular Birth of the
Christian Church

Acts 1–2

THE RUMORS FLEW AROUND JERUSALEM like leaves blowing in the wind. People were claiming that Jesus, the Jewish rabbi who had been executed at Passover, had come back to life and was appearing to his followers.

The high priest, Caiaphas, was frustrated to no end. Would these rumors never die? More than forty days had passed since he and the rest of the Sanhedrin had manipulated Governor Pilate into nailing this troublemaker to a Roman cross. The threat Jesus had posed to their control over the Jews should have died with him. But after his buried body had gone missing, hundreds of people throughout Judea and Galilee claimed to have seen him alive, and the rumors wouldn't stop. The authorities knew the only way to get people to quiet down about Jesus was to produce his body and parade it through Jerusalem. But that body was nowhere to be found.

Meanwhile, Jesus' disciples knew their lives were in danger. If the

Jewish authorities couldn't produce a body, their next move would be to silence Jesus' followers. And as their ruthless treatment of Jesus indicated, they would use any means necessary to do so. Shortly after the Resurrection, the disciples had fled to Galilee for safety. But the risen Jesus had met them there and told them to return to Jerusalem, saying they would be baptized "in just a few days" (Acts 1:5). He told them to wait there for his power to come upon them. They understood little of what he said, yet they obeyed and went back to Jerusalem. Knowing that danger lurked there, they banded together for protection and remained in hiding.

The risen Jesus remained on earth for forty days, and then he ascended into heaven ten days before the Jewish observance of Pentecost. Pentecost, one of the most sacred of Israel's holy days, brought Jews and Jewish converts from all over the world to Jerusalem. Parthians, Medes, Mesopotamians, Cappadocians, Asians, Phrygians, Pamphylians, Cretans, Romans, Arabs, and travelers from many other nations assembled in Jerusalem to celebrate.

Caiaphas and Pilate knew that such a collection of people groups could be volatile, especially with the uncertainties about Jesus still lingering. The turmoil that had plagued the Roman authorities at Passover could all too easily erupt again.

Waiting in Jerusalem

The disciples of Jesus banded together to wait as Jesus had instructed. They occupied a large upper room—probably in the home of a wealthy disciple—that would accommodate 120 people, including the 11 remaining apostles and Mary, the mother of Jesus.

Waiting was hard for these disciples—especially for Peter, who always preferred to act rather than wait. However, they were no longer a moping, grieving, and discouraged lot as they had been right after the Crucifixion. They were energized by Jesus' resurrection and his promise of coming power.

What was this power? As they awaited further instructions, they no doubt asked this question over and over. But no one knew the answer. As their initial reaction to Jesus' promise indicates, they still thought he was planning to drive out the Romans and establish Jewish independence (Acts 1:6). This coming power was surely some phenomenon that would enable them to accomplish that feat.

Would the power be a type of military force? Would it be supernatural? God had fought for Israel with divine intervention in the past. When the Egyptian pharaoh refused to free the enslaved Israelite nation, God crushed Egypt with ten devastating plagues (Exodus 1–12). On another occasion, he endowed the Israelite judge Samson with superhuman physical strength, enabling him to single-handedly kill one thousand Philistines (Judges 15:14-16). God also led Israel's hero Gideon to defeat a massive Midianite army of many thousands with only three hundred men (Judges 7:1-25).

God had performed such wonders before, and he could do it again. Small numbers or lack of training did not matter. Whatever

THE FEAST OF PENTECOST

The word *Pentecost* is the Greek name for the Jewish festival Shavuot. Pentecost celebrated two coinciding events, one ancient and the other ongoing. The first marked the occasion of Moses receiving the Ten Commandments on Mount Sinai, which had occurred seven weeks after the original Passover in Egypt. The second event was the culmination of the Feast of Weeks. This feast derived its name from the seven-week harvest of wheat and barley, which began at Passover. The day after this seven-week harvest was designated as a time of celebration and thanks to God, which the Jews expressed by bringing an offering of the first crops from their harvests to the Temple. Since that was the fiftieth day after Passover, it was called Pentecost, meaning "fifty days."

was ahead, the disciples were ready. But to their credit, they didn't rush to conclusions or take impulsive actions. Instead, "they all met together and were constantly united in prayer" (Acts 1:14).

Though they were eager to be part of advancing the Kingdom Jesus had talked about, they were not about to get ahead of their master's leading. Like good soldiers, they would obey. It is likely that their prayers went something like this: "Lord, prepare us to accomplish your will so that when your power comes, we'll be ready to go out and do whatever you require."

Peter, always driven to action, found a task to keep the disciples occupied as they waited. He reminded the group that Jesus had originally chosen twelve men to be his apostles—a select, inner circle of disciples. Now that one of these men, Judas, had become a traitor and ended his own life, it was time to select a replacement.

The group nominated two men, Joseph Barsabbas and Matthias, as the most qualified candidates to fill the vacancy. Before moving forward with the final selection, they prayed, "O Lord, you know every heart. Show us which of these men you have chosen as an apostle to replace Judas in this ministry, for he has deserted us and gone where he belongs" (Acts 1:24-25). Then, using an ancient method often employed to discern the will of God, "they cast lots, and Matthias was selected to become an apostle with the other eleven" (Acts 1:26). With the number of apostles again complete, the group continued their waiting.

The Arrival of the Holy Spirit

On the morning of Pentecost, the 120 disciples, including the 12 apostles, were in the upper room, still waiting. Then it happened. A deafening roar startled them—like the sound of a rushing wind. It filled the entire house and shocked the crowds of people heading to the Temple to celebrate Pentecost. Then bright streaks of light resembling flaming tongues flashed above each of the disciples as the Holy Spirit entered into them.

THE APOSTLES

The apostles were the twelve men Jesus chose as his closest companions and pupils. He trained them to spread the gospel and lead the church after his ascension. Each apostle had to meet certain criteria: (1) he had to have been an eyewitness to the entire ministry of Jesus (Acts 1:21); (2) he had to have encountered the resurrected Jesus (Acts 1:22); and (3) he had to be selected by God himself (Acts 1:24).

Their waiting was over. The power Jesus had promised had finally come.

Their fear vanished, and these ignited disciples rushed out into the streets and stood before the astonished group of spectators that had gathered. They began to talk and found themselves speaking fluently in foreign languages they had never studied. Everyone in the crowd heard the disciples speaking in his or her own tongue.

No one knew what to make of this astounding event. Some people realized that a miracle was taking place. They knew these blue-collar Galileans were not likely to be able to speak any language other than their own, much less the wide range of languages represented in this mass of people. Scripture says, "They stood there amazed and perplexed. 'What can this mean?' they asked each other" (Acts 2:12).

Others, however, were not so open to this work of God and scoffed at the disciples. "They're just drunk, that's all!" they cried, apparently ignoring the fact that being drunk does not enable fluency in an unknown language (Acts 2:13).

The bold apostle Peter stepped up and addressed the crowd, saying that they had not been drinking and reminding the crowd that it was only nine o'clock in the morning (Acts 2:15). On festival days, Jews were not allowed to break their fast until the fourth hour, or ten o'clock. Peter was making the claim that the disciples could not be drunk because it was too early for a Jew to eat or drink on this holy day.

The Sermon That Birthed the Church

Now that the disciples had the crowd's attention, Peter began to preach what was certainly the most powerful sermon heard since Jesus' Sermon on the Mount. At the outset, he addressed the people's wonder by telling them that the miracle they were witnessing had been prophesied in the book of Joel: "I will pour out my Spirit upon all people. Your sons and daughters will prophesy. Your old men will dream dreams, and your young men will see visions. In those days I will pour out my Spirit even on servants—men and women alike. . . . Everyone who calls on the name of the LORD will be saved" (Joel 2:28-29, 32). The people in Peter's audience, being observant Jews, would have recognized this prophecy and seen its connection to the event they were witnessing.

Once Peter had given context for what the people had just seen, he plunged directly into the heart of his sermon. He proclaimed that through miracles, signs, and wonders, God had made it clear to the Jews that Jesus was Israel's Messiah. Then he did something that few preachers in our day would dare to do. He confronted his audience with a serious accusation: "With the help of lawless Gentiles, you nailed [Jesus] to a cross and killed him" (Acts 2:23). Not the textbook way for a preacher to win over an audience. But the bold step got their attention. These Jews knew what Peter was talking about. Every person there had heard the story of Jesus' crucifixion and rumors of his resurrection many times since arriving in Jerusalem.

Peter went on to say that the Resurrection was no mere rumor. He quoted and explained a psalm of David that prophesied that

SPEAKING IN TONGUES

When the Holy Spirit descended at Pentecost, the disciples "began to speak with other tongues" (Acts 2:4, NKJV). This was human speech in recognizable languages. We know this to be true because everyone was amazed to "hear their own languages being spoken by the believers" (Acts 2:6). This does not mean that the disciples spoke in their native language and the Holy Spirit translated it into the language of each listener. The miracle was not in the hearers; it was in the speakers.

Jesus' soul would not remain among the dead, nor would his body be abandoned in the grave (Psalm 16:10). God would raise Jesus up and take him into heaven to sit at God's right hand, and Jesus' enemies would become his footstool (Acts 2:35).

Far from riling up the crowd in defensive anger, Peter's words "pierced their hearts" (Acts 2:37). Peter had painted a pretty grim picture of their part in this drama. God had sent the Messiah they had anticipated for centuries, and they had killed him. Now he wielded all the power of heaven and was poised to crush his enemies under his feet. That meant every one of the people within earshot of the disciples.

Some anguished souls in the audience cried out, "Brothers, what should we do?" (Acts 2:37).

Peter replied, "Each of you must repent of your sins and turn to God, and be baptized in the name of Jesus Christ for the forgiveness of your sins. Then you will receive the gift of the Holy Spirit" (Acts 2:38).

About three thousand people responded to the call and were baptized that day. Rarely, if ever, has a sermon been so effective, and its effects spread exponentially. Each person who received this message was filled with the Holy Spirit. Then, spreading like wildfire, these people returned to their homes throughout the nations and passed the flame along to others, who in turn passed it to still others. It was a spectacular initiation of the charge Jesus gave his disciples just before his ascension: "Go and make disciples of all the nations, baptizing them in the name of the Father and the Son and the Holy Spirit" (Matthew 28:19).

The disciples were no longer befuddled about their mission. They now realized that they had been wearing blinders when it came to the kind of Kingdom that Jesus was establishing. Jesus' mission was not merely to save Israel from the Romans; it was to save the world from Satan. He was not merely the Messiah to the Jews; he was the Messiah to people in all nations around the globe. He was the rightful King not of just the Jews but of the whole world, which since the time of Adam and Eve had been "enemy-occupied territory."[1] The task of these disciples was to lead people out from under the tyranny of a demonic usurper and rally them around the flag of a resistance movement led by Jesus Christ, their true King.

The power Jesus had promised was infinitely better than anything they could have anticipated. It filled them with more joy and love and courage than they had ever imagined possible.

WHAT DOES THE WORD *CHRIST* MEAN?

The word *Christ* comes from a Greek word meaning "savior, deliverer, or anointed one." The term *Jesus Christ* is not the first and last name of Jesus, as it might seem. Instead, it is a title meaning "Jesus, the Anointed One" or "Jesus, the Deliverer." This title applies exclusively to Jesus, the Son of God, indicating his role as the world's Savior and anointed King.

✢ ✢ ✢

The New Beginning

The New Testament book known as Acts is shorthand for the full title: the Acts of the Apostles. It chronicles the beginning of the Christian church, which initiates a new beginning for all of humanity. It is also the story of the Holy Spirit, who is the power behind this new beginning. Acts is one of the most gripping books of the Bible, filled with adventure, heroism, danger, narrow escapes, and tragic deaths. But the birth of the church isn't just a historical event; it also has implications for us thousands of years later.

The Holy Spirit

Without the Holy Spirit, there would be no Christianity and no Christian church. Yet many people think of the Holy Spirit as a ghost or an imaginary character. They assume that because he can't be seen or touched, he doesn't even exist. To understand just who the Holy Spirit is and what he does, we must explore his nature.

THE HOLY SPIRIT IS A PERSON

The Holy Spirit is not an impersonal force, but a person. Psychologists tell us that the attributes of personality are threefold: a person must have intellect, emotion, and will. It is not surprising, then, to discover that the Holy Spirit possesses each of these attributes.

He possesses intellect: he knows the thoughts and heart of God. "No one can know a person's thoughts except that person's own spirit, and no one can know God's thoughts except God's own Spirit" (1 Corinthians 2:11).

The Holy Spirit also possesses emotion. Our actions can grieve him (Ephesians 4:30). The apostle Paul wrote, "I urge you in the name of our Lord Jesus Christ to join in my struggle by praying to God for me. Do this because of your love for me, given to you by the Holy Spirit" (Romans 15:30). The Holy Spirit loves and knows sorrow; therefore, he has emotion.

Finally, the Holy Spirit possesses will. Consider 1 Corinthians 12:11: "It is the one and only Spirit who distributes all these gifts. He alone decides which gift each person should have." In other words, he has particular desires and chooses to act in certain ways.

THE HOLY SPIRIT IS GOD

Although the Holy Spirit is an equal member of the Trinity, many people do not view the Holy Spirit as God. They consider him to be almost God, but not quite. In the Bible, however, there is no ambiguity. Here are four key ways Scripture clearly shows that the Holy Spirit is God.

First, the Holy Spirit is called God in the Bible. One account in the book of Acts clearly illustrates his deity. Ananias and his wife had lied to the apostles about money they were giving to the church. Peter said, "Ananias, why have you let Satan fill your heart? You lied to the Holy Spirit, and you kept some of the money for yourself. . . . You weren't lying to us but to God" (Acts 5:3-4). Peter used "the Holy Spirit" at the beginning of the statement and "God" at the end. This truth is clearly stated in 2 Corinthians 3:17: "The Lord is the Spirit."

Second, the Holy Spirit is associated with God in the Bible. In Matthew 28:19, Jesus tells his disciples to "go and make disciples of all the nations, baptizing them in the name of the Father and the Son and the Holy Spirit." The Holy Spirit is closely connected to both the Father and the Son in this benediction: "May the grace of the Lord Jesus Christ, the love of God, and the fellowship of the Holy Spirit be with you all" (2 Corinthians 13:14).

Third, the Holy Spirit performs the actions of God. Everything God does, the Holy Spirit does. God creates and gives life; the Holy Spirit creates and gives life (Genesis 1:1-2; John 3:5-7; Romans 8:11). God performs miracles; the Holy Spirit performs miracles (Matthew 12:28; 1 Corinthians 12:9). Everything that only God can do, the Holy Spirit does.

Finally, the Holy Spirit has all the attributes of God. He is omnipotent. He is omniscient. He is omnipresent. He is holy. He is wise. Everything we say about God, we can say about the Holy Spirit (Psalm 139:7-8; 1 Corinthians 2:10-11; 1 Peter 3:18).

The Spirit-Empowered Church

When the Holy Spirit of God descended on Pentecost and entered the disciples, they continued Jesus Christ's work as bearers of the life of God on earth. This event marked a new beginning for humanity. On that day, God began restoring human beings to their original created purpose.

These early believers "devoted themselves to the apostles' teaching, and to fellowship, and to sharing in meals (including the Lord's Supper), and to prayer" (Acts 2:42). With these actions, they demonstrated what it means to be a church, united in one purpose by one Spirit to function as the body of Christ (1 Corinthians 12:12-27).

THE APOSTLES' TEACHING

Theologian James Montgomery Boice makes an interesting observation about the priority of teaching in the early church:

> There were a lot of . . . things Luke could have said about
> it. As we go on, we find that it was a joyful church, also
> an expanding, vibrant church. These are important items.
> Nevertheless, the first thing Luke talks about is the teaching.
> He stresses that in these early days, in spite of an experience
> as great as that of Pentecost, which might have caused
> them to focus on their experiences, the disciples devoted
> themselves first to teaching.[2]

It is also important to observe what the early church was studying: the apostles' doctrine. The apostles were those who had witnessed the life of Christ. They had been firsthand observers of his ministry, death, resurrection, and ascension, and it was their words that were being taught in the early church. Those are the truths that continue to be the core teaching for believers to this day. It's exciting to know that the doctrine that was taught to the early believers after Pentecost is now available to us in the New Testament.

Isolation, loneliness, and fractured relationships are some of the defining characteristics of contemporary Western culture. Divorce rates have soared to around 50 percent. More than one-fourth of American children are reared by single parents, and untold numbers of children suffer at the hands of abusive or neglectful parents. The Internet and social media provide tools for building relationships, but people are hungrier than ever for meaningful, authentic, and life-giving friendships.

The church, the body of Christ, offers the antidote to this malady. It offers solutions to the problems of loneliness, fractured relationships, isolation, and emptiness. The early church was known for taking its mission of community seriously. Here are some of the hallmarks of fellowship in the early church.

The Church Opened Its Hearts

The New Testament word for fellowship is *koinonia*. It can be translated "partnership" or "sharing," and it has an implication of holding things in common. The Christian life is not to be lived in isolation, but with other believers and with God. "We proclaim to you what we ourselves have actually seen and heard so that you may have fellowship with us. And our fellowship is with the Father and with his Son, Jesus Christ" (1 John 1:3).

The Spirit-empowered church is a place where we can experience the radical acceptance we see in the gospel, sharing the best and the worst of ourselves with one another. The apostle Paul writes, "Accept each other just as Christ has accepted you" (Romans 15:7). Pastor R. Kent Hughes explains the meaning of this verse:

> How did Christ accept you and me? He accepted us with our many sins, prejudices, and innumerable blind spots. He accepted us with our psychological shortcomings and cultural naiveté. He accepted us with our provincialisms. He even accepted us with our stubbornness. This is how we are to accept one another.[3]

The early Christians enfolded one another in their hearts. Today, twenty centuries later, the church is still intended to model the same kind of mutual love and fellowship. Authentic churches offer a community built on love, support, and acceptance.

The Church Opened Its Hands

In the early church, "all the believers met together in one place and shared everything they had. They sold their property and possessions and shared the money with those in need" (Acts 2:44-45). The fledgling church experienced severe persecution, leaving members displaced and destitute. They formed a close-knit community to take care of one another, sharing their food, clothing, and money to meet people's needs.

Over the years, some people have pointed to this passage to make the claim that the early church practiced Communism or socialism, but such was not the case. Communism is a compulsory sharing of goods because no one is thought to have the right to own anything. Socialism acknowledges the right of private property, but it requires individuals to give a certain percentage of what they earn to others in order to narrow the gap between socioeconomic classes.

The early church, however, shared their goods because they were generous and committed to one another. Scripture doesn't say that the entire church sold all they had and gave everything up for the community's welfare. It simply says that people voluntarily sold their possessions as financial concerns arose and gave the proceeds to those in need.

Today, almost every church takes care to meet the needs of members lacking food, shelter, help, or clothing. Some churches have food banks or centers offering furniture and clothing. The authentic church is a caring and generous community.

The Church Opened Its Homes

The early Christians were hospitable and invited one another into their homes. They "met in homes . . . and shared their meals with great joy and generosity" (Acts 2:46). Hospitality is a prevalent theme in the New Testament. For instance, in Romans 12:13 we are told that all Christians are to show hospitality. Titus 1:8 says that hospitality is a requirement for anyone who would serve as an elder. And Hebrews 13:2 instructs us to welcome strangers, because by doing so we might entertain angels without being aware of it. Max Lucado writes,

> Long before the church had pulpits and baptisteries, she had kitchens and dinner tables. . . . Even a casual reading of the New Testament unveils the house as the primary tool of the church. . . . The primary gathering place of the church was the home.
>
> Something holy happens around a dinner table that will never happen in a sanctuary. In a church auditorium you see the backs of heads. Around the table you see the expressions on faces. In the auditorium one person speaks; around the table everyone has a voice. Church services are on the clock. Around the table there is time to talk.
>
> Hospitality opens the door to uncommon community. It's no accident that *hospitality* and *hospital* come from the

same Latin word, for they both lead to the same result: healing. When you open your door to someone, you are sending this message: "You matter to me and to God." You may think you are saying, "Come over for a visit." But what your guest hears is, "I'm worth the effort."[4]

One of my fondest memories from my childhood as a pastor's kid is the constant parade of people God brought through our home. I remember coming home from school and my mother often saying to me, "David, you are not sleeping in your bed tonight. We are having guests. You get to sleep on the couch."

I can't ever remember being sorry about that, because the guests who came were always interesting people. I enjoyed listening to their life stories, and they made a profound impact on me.

In most churches today, members meet regularly in one another's homes, whether in small groups or informal gatherings. These meetings offer intimate fellowship that may include studying the Bible, sharing victories and failures, supporting and encouraging one another, and sharing meals together. Not only do such groups provide satisfying social connections, they also offer a deep connection with others who share a common spiritual bond. The church offers family—a caring community where people can find love and belonging.

PRAYER

Finally, the first Christian church devoted itself to prayer. This is not a reference to private prayers as much as to the public prayers that were offered as believers gathered together.

Theologian J. C. Macaulay describes what these times of prayer might have looked like: "The prayers were a carefully guarded exercise of the assembly, when they thoughtfully and earnestly worshiped God, adoring His glorious being, confessing their sins, petitioning His grace, and giving hearty thanks for the multitude of His mercies."[5]

This new group of believers prayed all sorts of prayers. They prayed prayers of praise, thanks, petition, and confession; they prayed extemporaneous prayers as well as formal memorized prayers from their Jewish backgrounds. These latter prayers were offered with a whole new meaning and context as they incorporated Old Testament truths into a New Testament understanding of the death and resurrection of Christ.

English pastor John Stott summarizes the characteristics of the early church with these words about the priority of relationships:

> Looking back over these marks of the first Spirit-filled community, it is evident that they all concerned the church's relationships. First, they were related to the apostles (in submission). They were eager to receive the apostles' instruction. A Spirit-filled church is an apostolic church, a New Testament church, anxious to believe and obey what Jesus and his apostles taught.
>
> Secondly, they were related to each other (in love). They persevered in the fellowship, supporting each other and relieving the needs of the poor. A Spirit-filled church is a loving, caring, sharing church.
>
> Thirdly, they were related to God (in worship). They worshipped him in the temple and in the home, in the Lord's Supper and in the prayers, with joy and with reverence. A Spirit-filled church is a worshipping church.
>
> Fourthly, they were related to the world (in outreach). They were engaged in continuous evangelism. No self-centred, self-contained church (absorbed in its own parochial affairs) can claim to be filled with the Spirit. The Holy Spirit is a missionary Spirit. So a Spirit-filled church is a missionary church.[6]

The Growth of the Church

The lives and prayers of the early church were so powerful that everyone who observed them experienced a sense of awe. This was not an awe over the buildings or the budgets or the programs but rather an awe of the almighty God and his obvious presence within the fellowship.

The church grew and found favor with all the people—those inside the church and those outside. Their love for one another was a testimony even to those who did not agree with what they were preaching. The church grew not only in depth but also in breadth: "Each day the Lord added to their fellowship those who were being saved" (Acts 2:47). The following numbers and descriptive terms are given to us in the book of Acts concerning the growth of the church (emphasis has been added).

- "About *120* believers were together in one place" (Acts 1:15).
- "Those who believed what Peter said were baptized and added to the church that day—about *3,000* in all" (Acts 2:41).
- "The number of believers . . . totaled about *5,000* men, not counting women and children" (Acts 4:4).
- "*More and more* people believed" (Acts 5:14).
- "The number of believers *greatly increased*" (Acts 6:7).
- "*Many* believed" (Acts 9:42).
- "*A large number* . . . believed" (Acts 11:21).
- "*A great number* . . . became believers" (Acts 14:1).
- "*Many* Jews believed, as did *many* of the prominent Greek women and men" (Acts 17:12).
- "Paul . . . persuaded *many* people that handmade gods aren't really gods at all. And he's done this not only here in Ephesus but *throughout the entire province!*" (Acts 19:26).
- "*Many thousands* . . . believed" (Acts 21:20).

A Place to Belong

In Charlotte Brontë's classic novel *Jane Eyre*, the heroine, Jane, has suffered one rejection after another throughout her young life. She was orphaned as a baby, abused by her adoptive family, and sent to a boarding school where she suffered further abuse and deprivation. Upon graduation, she becomes a governess and falls in love with her employer, whom she eventually leaves when she finds out he has deceived her. Destitute and friendless, she wanders, half starved, to a poor community where she ekes out a living as a schoolteacher.

Then one day Jane receives a letter. A wealthy uncle she didn't even know she had has died and left her his fortune, making her independently wealthy. The letter also says that three members of the community are her second cousins. She is so elated to find that she has a real family that the news of her new wealth hardly registers with her. She learns that these newfound relatives inherited nothing, and without hesitation, she shares her fortune equally with them. The money means nothing to her, while finding she is part of a real family means everything.

Everyone needs family. Everyone needs a community where they can experience love and sharing. Everyone needs a place to belong. The church provides just that. Jesus himself offered the invitation that so many hurting people long to hear: "Come to me, all of you who are weary and carry heavy burdens, and I will give you rest" (Matthew 11:28). Today, through his church, he renews that invitation and offers relief from the burdens that weigh on our souls, including the grief, loneliness, fractured relationships, and isolation that are so prevalent. If you lack a father's love, God will be your Father. If you need a friend, Jesus will be your friend. If you long for a family, the church will be your family.

The church was born on Pentecost when God made his Spirit available to those who opened themselves to him. He is still available today, and you can be one of those disciples who live by his dynamic power and enjoy the love he pours into you.

CHAPTER 4

OPPORTUNITY AND OPPOSITION

✦ ✦ ✦

The New Movement Gets a Foothold

Acts 3–4

Jews in Jerusalem had grown so accustomed to the beggar's presence that they hardly even noticed him. For as long as most could remember, he had been carried to the Temple gate every morning, where he sat asking for money all day. The poor man had little choice but to beg. He had been born paralyzed, and his legs were atrophied and useless. In his forty years of life, he had never taken a single step. He was a fixture of the Temple, and like old, familiar fixtures, he was easily overlooked. Those who dropped coins into his cup rarely even glanced at him.

This man had been intentional about the location of his begging spot. People coming to the Temple often brought money to put into the Temple treasury, and some of them thought that a bit of charity for the poor would impress God—or perhaps, impress those who were watching. That generosity usually consisted of nothing more than a shekel or two dropped into the cup—with enough force to ensure that the clank of the coins would broadcast their good deeds.

Three o'clock in the afternoon would have been a peak hour for the paralyzed man. It was the customary time for Jewish prayer, and traffic to the Temple picked up considerably. Waving his cup, he looked up woefully at the stream of passing worshipers. As usual, most ignored him. Then he noticed two men who seemed to be angling through the crowd toward him. Hoping to get a handout, he thrust his cup forward and pleaded for money.

But instead of reaching for a money pouch, the two men gazed at him intently. Then one of them said, "Look at us!" (Acts 3:4).

The man couldn't help but look. No one had ever tried to connect with him in this way. Surely they were about to drop a considerable sum into his cup, and they apparently wanted his complete focus on their generosity. But their next words deflated his expectations like a ruptured wineskin.

"I don't have any silver or gold for you," said the spokesman for the two (who was none other than Peter, accompanied by his fellow apostle John). "But I'll give you what I have. In the name of Jesus Christ the Nazarene, get up and walk!" (Acts 3:6).

Peter reached down, took the man by the hand, and pulled him to his feet. At that moment, the astonished beggar received the shock of his life. Immediately he felt sensation and strength flow into his useless legs. Muscles expanded. Sinews grew firm. Bones hardened. Blood pulsed through previously collapsed arteries. The coordination to walk miraculously flowed from his cerebral cortex to the nerves in his legs.

The man leaped to his feet, unable to contain his elation. He entered the Temple with Peter and John—not just ambling along, but leaping, dancing, and shouting praise to God.

The people in the Temple turned toward the commotion and gaped with amazement. It was the crippled beggar they had passed at the gate for decades—healed, healthy, whole, and deliriously happy! They didn't know how to process the seeming impossibility of what they saw. Clearly, a miracle had occurred.

As the stunned crowd gathered around, Peter did what any good preacher would do. With such a receptive audience looking for answers, he preached. And what a sermon it was!

First, Peter deflected the glory for the miracle from himself to its true source. It was not he who had healed the man; it was the power of the risen Jesus working through him. Then, as he had done on the day of Pentecost, Peter ignored niceties and accused his audience of committing an atrocious crime. They had murdered Jesus, the Messiah who had been promised in their Scriptures. Yes, Peter acknowledged, they had done it out of ignorance, but ignorance was no excuse. The truth of who Jesus was had been made abundantly clear by his claims, his miracles, and the many prophecies he had

THE JEWISH TEMPLE

After the nation of Israel was established, King David drew plans and assembled materials for his son Solomon to build a permanent Temple to replace the portable Tabernacle. The Temple, completed in 959 B.C., was a wonder of the ancient world. To the great sadness of the Jewish nation, the Babylonians destroyed the Temple when they conquered and deported the Jews in 586 B.C. These Jewish exiles returned and rebuilt a much-inferior Temple in 515 B.C. In 20 B.C. Herod the Great expanded its size to rival Solomon's original Temple, adding expansive paved courts, porticos, gates, and a central tower housing the sacred inner chamber, the Holy of Holies. The unrestricted outer court became a popular meeting place, which is where the apostles would have seen the man begging. The Romans destroyed Jerusalem, including the Temple, in A.D. 70. It was never rebuilt.

fulfilled. It was a bitter accusation for his audience to swallow, but he knew that if they were to repent, they would first have to see themselves as guilty before God. The bad news was necessary to set up the good news.

Then, as he had done in his Pentecost sermon, Peter explained that God had raised Jesus from the dead. This meant that Jesus, whom they had killed, was now alive. His death had paid the price for their sin, and his resurrection had given them the hope of new life. To receive that new life, they needed to repent so their sin could be forgiven.

This second sermon of Peter's was another huge success. Scores of listeners throughout the Temple courts believed, joined the disciples, and carried this message to their families and neighbors, swelling the total number of disciples to more than five thousand (Acts 4:4).

Arrest, Interrogation, and Accusation

As Peter ended his sermon, the captain of the Temple guard pushed his way through the crowd and marched straight to Peter and John.

SADDUCEES AND PHARISEES

The Sadducees were an elite Jewish political and religious sect who were considered the liberals of their day. They cooperated with the Romans and rejected many orthodox Jewish beliefs, such as the existence of angels and spirits and the resurrection of the dead. The Pharisees were the opposing Jewish sect, and they believed in the spirit world and the resurrection of the dead. They strictly upheld the letter of the Jewish law, thinking that meticulous ritual observance would hasten the return of the Messiah. Jesus often rebuked the Pharisees for strictly observing ceremonial details while ignoring greater truths (Matthew 23:23).

Accompanying him were a group of priests and members of the Sadducees, a Jewish religious sect. Without explanation, they seized the two apostles and dragged them off to prison.

The typical prison cell of that day was not designed for comfort. It was cramped, filthy, and infested with vermin, and the only bed was a pile of rancid straw. After a long, sleepless night, the two apostles were hustled out of jail and marched into the chamber of the Sanhedrin, along with exhibit A, the healed beggar. They found themselves standing face-to-face with the seventy priests, scribes, and elders who served as the Jewish religious rulers. Also in attendance were the associates of Caiaphas, the high priest.

Caiaphas was already frustrated by his failure to put an end to Jesus' influence with the Crucifixion. Now the dead man's followers were claiming that he had been resurrected, and they were stirring up the people with his teachings. Caiaphas's first question to Peter and John got right to the heart of his concern: "By what power, or in whose name, have you done this?" (Acts 4:7)

Peter's mildly ironic but pointed reply displayed the inverted values of his accusers: "Are we being questioned today because we've done a good deed for a crippled man?" (Acts 4:9).

With that little barb firmly planted, Peter seized the opportunity to launch into another sermon. Jesus had told his disciples that they would be dragged before councils and accused, but that they should not worry about what they should say. They would be given the right words when they needed them (Mark 13:9-11). Peter's masterpiece of a sermon displayed the fulfillment of that prophecy. He began with a bold and unequivocal answer to the question Caiaphas had asked:

Let me clearly state to all of you and to all the people of Israel that he was healed by the powerful name of Jesus Christ the Nazarene, the man you crucified but whom God raised from the dead. For Jesus is the one referred to in the Scriptures, where it says, "The stone that you builders rejected has now become the cornerstone." There is salvation in no one else! God has given no other name under heaven by which we must be saved.   ACTS 4:10-12

Was this the same Peter who had cowered in the background when Jesus was arrested? The same man who had denied him three times to protect his own skin? Here he was, speaking to the very men who had condemned Jesus, accusing them of killing their own Messiah. The accused had become the accuser. This moment revealed a dramatic turnaround in Peter's character. He was now confident, assured, and unafraid to speak the truth in dangerous circumstances. He also demonstrated the quick wit and sharp reason he had lacked before.

What made the difference? The Holy Spirit.

In Peter's little sermon, which is only about ninety words long in the original Greek, this backwater fisherman dared to go head-to-head with the leading theologians of Israel. In accusing them of killing their Messiah, Peter drew on a prophecy from one of the psalms: "The stone that the builders rejected has now become the cornerstone" (Psalm 118:22).

As experts in theology, Peter's audience would have understood his point perfectly. They were familiar with this psalm, and they knew the significance of the metaphor he was using. A cornerstone was the foundational piece in a building's construction. It was the largest stone in the structure, and it was set in the corner so all the other stones could be aligned with it. These educated men knew what Peter was saying: Jesus of Nazareth was sent to be the cornerstone of God's new Kingdom—the one Israel had been charged with bringing to the rest of the world—and these leaders, who should have been the builders of that Kingdom, had cast the critical stone into the garbage heap. With these words of accusation, this fisherman—this nobody—reduced the smartest men in Israel to silence.

The Sanhedrin Reacts

The anger boiling up in the hearts of the Sanhedrin is almost palpable. How dare these uneducated fishermen lecture them—the nation's most prestigious leaders and scholars—on the finer points of theology! Adding insult to injury, Peter had again claimed that the resurrection of Jesus had really happened. They would not let this slide.

This should have been the big moment Caiaphas had been waiting for. He now had in his clutches the very men he'd been searching for—the ringleaders of Jesus' followers. It was in his power to crush them and squelch forever the troublesome rumor of Jesus' resurrection. Cut off the head, and this snake that threatened him would finally die.

But it wasn't that simple. Standing right before him was a man that everyone knew had been paralyzed his entire life but was now healthy and whole, healed in the name of the resurrected Jesus. It was obviously a miracle, and an astounding one. There was no way he could deny it.

Caiaphas and the Sadducees were bound by their misconceptions. They were convinced that there was no such thing as resurrection from the dead, yet here was proof that some living power had healed a man. Peter asserted that this power flowed from the risen Jesus. Rather than at least considering the possibility that Peter's claim might be true, they clung to their misconceptions like a miser to his purse and rejected reality in favor of their delusion.

The perplexed council sent Peter and John out of the room while they conferred. As desperate as they were to do away with these ringleaders of the early church, the undeniable fact of this miracle stood in their way. There was no doubt it was a real miracle, and the people knew it. How would the council look in the eyes of these people if they punished the ones responsible for this benevolent, miraculous act? Yet they were determined to find a way to stop the spread of this new movement.

The debate concluded with the decision to threaten Peter and John with severe consequences if they spoke about or performed healings in the name of Jesus again. The council knew that it was a weak solution, but it was the best they could come up with.

The leaders called Peter and John back into the chamber and commanded them to keep quiet about Jesus.

But Peter and John didn't waver. They replied, "Do you think God wants us to obey you rather than him? We cannot stop telling about everything we have seen and heard" (Acts 4:19-20).

The council was stunned. Outraged. Frustrated. Peter's question about whether they should obey God or human authority silenced them yet again. The Sanhedrin was responsible for interpreting God's laws for the people. Yet in this moment, the council showed once more their callous disregard for the law. They knew from the history of their people that when human law conflicts with God's, the believer is to disobey human authority and obey God.

When the nation of Israel was enslaved in Egypt, the Hebrew midwives disobeyed Pharaoh's decree to kill all the newborn male babies in the Israelite camp (Exodus 1). The prophet Daniel chose to be thrown into a den of hungry lions rather than obey the Babylonian king's order to pray to him (Daniel 6:1-10). Three Jewish exiles in Babylon—Shadrach, Meshach, and Abednego—would not worship a golden image of the king even though their refusal meant being cast into a blazing furnace (Daniel 3).

The members of the Sanhedrin were blind to the fact that these two apostles were following in the footsteps of those courageous heroes. And they—the very ones charged with upholding God's law—were the ones urging Peter and John to defy it.

We might expect the council to respond to such defiance by saying, "You ungrateful wretches! We gave you a chance to go free, but you blew it. Now it's back to prison for you, where you can rot until you come to your senses and listen to reason." But they couldn't do it. The people in the streets were already glorifying God because of the healing, and if this council punished the very people who performed the miracle, it would call into question the Sanhedrin's motives and undermine their power and influence.

In spite of the apostles' refusal to accept their terms, they had no choice but to set them free.

The Report and the Reaction

On leaving the Temple, Peter and John went directly back to their companions and reported everything that had happened to them, from their healing of the beggar to their release from the religious leaders' custody. When the other disciples heard this report, they recognized two things: first, the church was growing by leaps and bounds; second, persecution was now a constant threat. So the first thing they did was pray.

What did they pray for? Not what we would expect. We might assume they would pray that God would shield them from danger and prevent further opposition. But it seems that these thoughts never entered their minds. They already knew the danger they would face for proclaiming Christ. They were particularly aware of the prophecy from the Psalms, which predicted that the coming of Christ would drive rulers into a fury of opposition:

> Why are the nations so angry?
> Why do they waste their time with futile plans?
> The kings of the earth prepare for battle;
> the rulers plot together
> against the LORD
> and against his anointed one.
>
> PSALM 2:1-2

The disciples knew persecution would come, but to them it was not a deterrent. Instead of being fearful, they were filled with joy. They were grateful that Peter and John had been given the opportunity to preach the resurrection of Christ before the Jewish supreme court. This was not a cause for intimidation; it was a cause for celebration.

So instead of asking God for safety and protection, they prayed for greater boldness to meet these opportunities and face these challenges. They prayed not that God would let them off the hook but that he would empower them by his Holy Spirit to do even greater works.

As the inevitable persecution began, many of the believers were displaced or forced to go on the run to survive. The fledgling church again rose to the occasion and banded together to help one another. They shared their homes. Some donated land for others to live on. They sold property, houses, and other possessions and pooled their resources to ensure mutual survival. Scripture sums up the mind-set of the early church this way: "All the believers were united in heart and mind. And they felt that what they owned was not their own, so they shared everything they had. The apostles testified powerfully to the resurrection of the Lord Jesus, and God's great blessing was upon them all" (Acts 4:32-33).

✝ ✝ ✝

THE BEAUTY OF TOTAL COMMITMENT

When we read about Peter, John, and the burgeoning church in Acts 3 and 4, we can almost feel the tingle of excitement in the air. An enormous shift had been set in motion in the world. Everything about this movement was fresh and active and filled with the power infused into these believers by the Holy Spirit. They were unafraid, ready to proclaim the truth in the face of opposition and prepared to confront their adversaries when necessary. They were willing to suffer incarceration, loss of property, and even death. It seemed that the hotter things got, the more courageous they grew—and the better equipped they became to spread the word.

David Ben-Gurion, Israel's first prime minister, believed that "courage is a special kind of knowledge: the knowledge of how to fear what ought to be feared and how not to fear what ought not to be feared."[1] Nelson Mandela said that courage is "not the absence of fear, but the triumph over it. The brave man is not he who does not feel afraid, but he who conquers that fear."[2] And C. S. Lewis claimed that courage isn't just one virtue; rather, it is "the form of every virtue at the testing point, which means, at the point of highest reality."[3]

The Bible is filled with story after story of courageous men and women who stood for God even when it meant standing against all others.

Noah continued building the ark in spite of ridicule from his neighbors. What courage it must have taken for him and his family to be isolated from their entire community while building a structure unlike anything they had ever seen for a rain nobody had ever heard of! But Noah and his family persevered, simply because God told them to.

When twelve Israelite spies returned from their reconnaissance of the land of Canaan, Moses asked for their report. Ten of the spies said there was no way they could conquer the land: "The people living there are powerful, and their towns are large and fortified. We even saw giants there!" (Numbers 13:28). Joshua and Caleb stood against all the others and gave a courageous and honest report. Caleb said to the people, "Let's go at once to take the land. . . . We can certainly conquer it!" (Numbers 13:30).

David stood alone against the giant Goliath while his fellow soldiers cowered in fear. David had courage that came from a source beyond himself. He said to Goliath, "This is the LORD's battle, and he will give you to us" (1 Samuel 17:47). Then he bravely went out and defeated Goliath.

Esther boldly approached the king to save the lives of her people, knowing as she did so that she was putting her own life in danger.

God gave her the courage to do what was right, no matter the cost. "I will go in to see the king. If I must die, I must die" (Esther 4:16).

Throughout the Old and New Testaments, men and women of faith have dared to follow God even when it meant suffering or death.

Our Need for Boldness

The biblical record, including the book of Acts, delivers a timely message to the church in the United States. Opposition to the church and its beliefs is on the rise. We've already seen instances of suppression, and in my opinion, outright persecution is looming on the horizon. Widespread affluence and the availability of 24-7 entertainment have spawned a rapid decay of morality and ethics. We have reached the point in our culture where almost every kind of immorality is accepted and every belief must be tolerated—except Christianity and its biblical tenets.

Living in such an environment, it is easy for Christians to feel intimidated, to go along to get along, to soft-pedal their beliefs to avoid confrontation or ostracism. It's easy to water down Christianity and use it merely to help people live just a little better than they have been living. But the Christian's true calling is to lead people to know the authentic Christ, who demands the kind of radical transformation we see in these first chapters of Acts.

Peter didn't shy away from confrontation. He didn't pull any punches or try to be politically correct when he asserted one of the most profound, against-the-grain truths of the gospel. Speaking about Christ before the Sanhedrin, he said, "There is salvation in no one else! God has given no other name under heaven by which we must be saved" (Acts 4:12). There is hardly anything Christians can say today that causes more anger and opposition than that central and absolute truth.

Several years ago I spoke to some students at a university in New Jersey. In the question-and-answer session that followed, a man raised his hand. "Do you believe Jesus Christ is the only way to God?" he asked.

"It really doesn't make any difference what I think," I replied. "What really matters is what God says and what Jesus says. I don't want you to leave here thinking about what I believe. I want you to think about what God says in his Word. John 14:6 says, 'I am the way, the truth, and the life. No one can come to the Father except through me.'"

Scripture is filled with passages that teach this same truth.

- "This is the way to have eternal life—to know you, the only true God, and Jesus Christ, the one you sent to earth" (John 17:3).
- "There is salvation in no one else! God has given no other name under heaven by which we must be saved" (Acts 4:12).
- "There is one God and one Mediator who can reconcile God and humanity—the man Christ Jesus" (1 Timothy 2:5).

The truth that we can come to God only through Christ is a spiritual law that cannot be violated or changed. You might say with all sincerity, "I don't believe it," but that won't change reality one bit. There is no other way to God except through his Son, Jesus Christ.

Christians today must be willing to stand and proclaim this biblical truth in deep humility but without fear or apology. We can make this claim boldly and free from fear only by the power of the Holy Spirit—the same Holy Spirit who motivated the early Christians. So instead of praying for ease and safety, let's pray for the same type of boldness these early disciples possessed.

Whom Will We Obey?

When the Sanhedrin demanded that Peter stop preaching about Jesus, Peter shot back a telling question: "Do you think God wants us to obey you rather than him?" (Acts 4:19). At some point believers today will face this question as well. And as Western governments drift further away from godly principles, it will be something we face more often and with more serious consequences.

THE CHRISTIAN'S RESPONSIBILITY TO GOVERNMENT

Christ made it clear that we are obligated to obey civil law. The Pharisees once came to Jesus with this question: "Is it right to pay taxes to Caesar or not?"

When they showed him the coin used to pay the tax, he asked, "Whose picture and title are stamped on it?"

"Caesar's," they replied.

"Well, then," he responded, "give to Caesar what belongs to Caesar, and give to God what belongs to God" (Matthew 22:17-21).

In that single exchange, Jesus offered what might be the most significant political commentary ever made. He began by declaring the legitimacy of human governments. New Testament scholar James A. Brooks explains, "The coin that was minted by the emperor and had his image stamped on it was considered to be his personal property even while it was in circulation. Therefore it was proper for Jews and (later) Christians to return it to him. By so saying, Jesus acknowledged that God's people have an obligation to the state."[4] If we accept the government's privileges and protections, then we are obligated to support it.

The apostle Peter writes, "For the Lord's sake, submit to all human authority—whether the king as head of state, or the officials he has appointed. For the king has sent them to punish those who do wrong and to honor those who do right. . . . Fear God, and respect the king" (1 Peter 2:13-14, 17).

As these Scriptures show, governments have a legitimate and necessary function: to maintain an ordered society and provide defense for its citizens. Christians should be prime examples of obedience and respect for these authorities.

THE CHRISTIAN'S RESPONSIBILITY TO GOD

Although we have a calling to respect the government, there are limits to this kind of obedience. This is because God's authority is superior to any human authority: "Coins have the image of a ruler, and they may be returned to him. Human beings are made in the image of God; they and all they have belong to him."[5]

As Peter demonstrated in his comment to the Sanhedrin, when human law conflicts with God's law, Christians must obey God, even at personal risk. At times when civil disobedience is necessary, Christians should take care to go about it in a respectful way without resorting to self-righteousness and vitriol, and without displaying a martyr complex. This brings us back to our biblical examples of the Hebrew midwives, Daniel, and Daniel's three Hebrew friends. Although they refused to obey their leaders' edicts, they showed humility and respect to the authorities. In one instance, Daniel even came up with a creative alternative that preserved his integrity and prevented a confrontation (Daniel 1:8-16).

Because of my first birth, I am a citizen of the United States of America. And because of my second birth, I am a citizen of the Kingdom of God. Both involve very serious obligations.

Repentance: The Great Turnaround

Peter came down hard on the Jews who heard his sermon at the Temple gate, telling them they were guilty of killing the Messiah whom God had sent to save them. His intent was not spiteful or vindictive. But they had sinned, and sin carries a penalty. He knew they needed to face the truth of their guilt so they could accept the solution to it. Immediately after making the accusation, he gave them the solution: "Now repent of your sins and turn to God, so that your sins may be wiped away. Then times of refreshment will come from the presence of the Lord, and he will again send you Jesus, your appointed Messiah" (Acts 3:19-20).

Most people who have been exposed to Christianity understand that to be saved from the penalty of sin, one must believe. True enough, but there is more to belief than merely assenting to a fact. Authentic belief involves repentance. Without repentance, belief is an empty claim. Repentance does not mean, as some suppose, merely feeling sorry for one's sins. To simply confess sin, acknowledge Jesus Christ as the Son of God, and then continue life as it was is not authentic conversion. Repentance means turning around and going the other way. It means committing to a complete change in direction—to quit following oneself and start following Christ. Repentance is not a separate step in the conversion process; it is the essence of conversion and, indeed, of the entire Christian life.

One pastor describes the joy of repentance and its essential role in the Christian life: "Almost weekly, I ask people to repent. I ask them to change their minds, which is literally what repentance means. I invite them to see things God's way. To align themselves, stem to stern, with God's purposes. Initially that alignment is violent and dramatic, a 180-degree turn. But thereafter it's mostly course corrections—15 degrees here, 5 degrees there. But every turn, by whatever degree, is good news. Every turn moves us closer to where we want to be."[6]

In his sermon, Peter described four reasons for repentance.

1. **So that your sins might be wiped away.** Our sins have not been merely overlooked or pushed aside as if they were not serious; they have been completely taken away. They are no longer a part of us. They no longer stain our souls or make us guilty before God. As a result of repentance, those sins are gone forever (Acts 3:19).

2. **So that times of refreshment may come upon you.** Think about the euphoria we feel when a migraine headache goes

away, when a very sick child recovers, or when a large debt
is paid off. These are only dim previews of the relief and
refreshment that come when we are no longer weighed down
by the guilt we've carried for all our wrongs. We are free.
We are healed. A huge burden has been lifted. Our souls
are clean.

But the refreshment goes even beyond that. In the future,
when Christ returns, we will experience the refreshment of
the whole world when the Lord "will again send you Jesus,
your appointed Messiah" (Acts 3:20). It will be a world healed
fromevil, pain, death, and decay.

3. **So that you will escape judgment.** When Moses
    predicted that a prophet would come to judge all people
    (Deuteronomy 18:15), he was referring to Jesus. Peter told
    his audience, "Anyone who will not listen to that Prophet
    will be completely cut off from God's people" (Acts 3:23).
    Repentance means aligning your life with him now. Failure
    to repent means he will not recognize you as one of his own
    when he returns.

4. **So that you will experience God's blessing.** Peter, speaking
    to his Jewish listeners, says that God sent Jesus "to bless
    you by turning each of you back from your sinful ways"
    (Acts 3:26). That blessing is offered to us as well. The
    blessing of an all-new, unburdened, joyful, and deeply
    blessed life in Christ is available to everyone, regardless
    of race or gender or background, who repents and turns
    to him.

CHAPTER 5

HYPOCRITES AND HEROES

✝ ✝ ✝

Deception, Persecution, and Multiplication in the Early Church

Acts 4:36–5:42

AMONG THE NEW MEMBERS of the rapidly expanding church in Jerusalem was a man named Joseph who was from the Mediterranean island of Cyprus. Joseph always saw the best in everyone and never missed a chance to encourage the downhearted or comfort the hurting. This endearing trait led the apostles to give Joseph the nickname Barnabas, which means "Son of Encouragement." The name stuck, and throughout the rest of Acts he is never called Joseph again.

When persecution began to leave some of the believers destitute and homeless, Barnabas sold his land and brought all the proceeds to the apostles to be distributed to those in need. It was a selfless deed of love, for which Barnabas sought no glory. His gift endeared him even more to the believers.

Also among the new converts was a man named Ananias, who had some degree of wealth. After seeing the adulation heaped on

Barnabas and others who sold their property for the common good, Ananias decided to get in on the action. He had a parcel of land to sell, and he figured that donating the proceeds would elevate his status and give him an air of spiritual commitment.

Ananias got a good price for his land—enough that no one would suspect anything if he kept a significant sum for himself while claiming he was donating the entire amount. He let his wife, Sapphira, in on the deception, and she agreed to it.

Scripture doesn't give much detail about what happened next, but here's how I picture the scene. Ananias marched through the crowd of believers, the large bundle of coins jingling as he carried it openly for all to see. He reached the place where volunteers were handling the collections under the supervision of the apostles.

"See what I've brought?" he said. "I sold my land, just like Barnabas did. Here is the entire sum I received from it." With an elaborate gesture, he laid the heavy bag among the baskets.

Murmurs of admiration rippled throughout the room.

It worked, Ananias thought. *And no one will ever know the truth about this gift.*

But he was wrong—dead wrong. He thought he had hidden the truth, but nothing is hidden from God, who knows every thought harbored in the human heart (Psalm 44:21). At that moment, the Holy Spirit revealed Ananias's deception to the apostle Peter.

Peter looked straight at Ananias and said, "Why have you let Satan fill your heart? You lied to the Holy Spirit, and you kept some of the money for yourself. The property was yours to sell or not sell, as you wished. And after selling it, the money was also yours to give away. How could you do a thing like this? You weren't lying to us but to God!" (Acts 5:3-4). His sin was not that he had kept part of the price for himself; that was entirely his decision. His sin was deception.

Imagine the shock on Ananias's face in that moment. How could

WHAT IS A HYPOCRITE?

The word *hypocrite* comes from a Greek word that means "play actor." It has come to mean a person who feigns some virtue he or she does not truly uphold in order to be admired by others. No doubt the church has its share of religious hypocrites who put on a godly front that belies their inner character. But some behavior that may be labeled hypocrisy is not that at all. To act better than you feel like acting is not hypocrisy; it is an act of discipline to bring yourself into alignment with the standard you believe in. What God won't tolerate is true hypocrisy: when people intentionally try to deceive him or other people so they can receive affirmation for being good.

Peter possibly have known? But before Ananias could reply, he collapsed to the ground, dead. At Peter's signal, several young men wrapped the body and took it out to be buried.

When Ananias failed to return home, Sapphira set out to look for him. She knew where he had gone, so she went directly to the apostles and made an inquiry. But instead of revealing the fate of her husband, Peter asked Sapphira if Ananias had sold the land for the price he had claimed.

"Yes," she affirmed. "That was the price."

Peter replied, "How could the two of you even think of conspiring to test the Spirit of the Lord like this? The young men who buried your husband are just outside the door, and they will carry you out, too" (Acts 5:9).

Immediately Sapphira collapsed and died, just as Ananias had. The same young men took her body and buried it beside the body of her husband.

A Wave of Fear and a Resurgence of Power

The church reeled with shock at the deaths of Ananias and Sapphira. New converts had been drawn into this community of believers as a result of the apostles' healings and their preaching on Jesus' forgiveness of sin. To have two of their fellow believers suddenly struck down was the last thing they'd expected. No doubt some people started having second thoughts and slipped away, going back to their previous lives. They didn't want to be the next victims of God's judgment.

But these two deaths ultimately had a positive impact on the church, as the incident seems to have had a purifying effect. It instigated a sort of unofficial screening process, culling out those who were not fully committed to Jesus. Those who were barely hanging on dropped away, while those who remained were willing to subject their lives to the scrutiny of truth and take on all the risks of being believers.

The fear incited by these two deaths also spread to outsiders. While many people held the new church in high esteem because of the changed lives of its members, for a while "no one else dared to join them" (Acts 5:13). No doubt the apostles were concerned about this pause in the spread of the gospel, for immediately after this incident they went to the Temple, where they resumed their ministry and performed miraculous healings.

News of these miracles spread far past the walls of Jerusalem, and soon people who were sick, lame, impaired, and demon possessed began flocking to the city to be healed. Crowds surged into the city, and those who couldn't get close to the apostles lined the streets nearby, hoping Peter's passing shadow would bring healing (Acts 5:15).

The Opposition Strikes Again

When Caiaphas, the high priest, learned that massive crowds were gathering around the apostles once again, he seethed with anger. Would this Jesus problem never end? Killing the man himself should have brought things to a halt, but now his disciples were generating the same kind of trouble. Caiaphas had tried to silence them with threats, which had only spurred them to redouble their efforts. It was as if Jesus had never died but was somehow present within the lives of his disciples.

Caiaphas and the Sadducees again faced the problem that had prompted them to arrest Peter and John not long before. These Jesus followers were winning the hearts of the people. And they were doing so largely by performing miracles, thus exhibiting a real power these council members lacked. Not only were these Jewish leaders green with jealousy, but their Sadducee doctrines were also being threatened. How could they keep the people believing that there was no supernatural realm while the apostles were performing miracles by some power beyond themselves? How could they keep them believing that there was no resurrection when the apostles were claiming they performed these miracles by the power of the resurrected Jesus?

One might think that in the face of such an obvious demonstration of God's power, these leaders would finally reexamine their beliefs. But their hearts were hardened to the truth, and they didn't have the humility to accept that their entire system of theology might be flawed. Their solution was not to seek the truth but to kill the opposition. Yes, killing the apostles would upset many people, but the alternative was to watch their own influence unravel like a fraying rope.

Caiaphas ordered the Temple police to go out and seize Peter and John and hold them for arraignment the following morning. The police "laid their hands on the apostles and put them in the common prison" (Acts 5:18, NKJV), meaning they roughed them up and dragged them off to jail.

The iron doors were slammed shut, and guards were posted at the gate. The apostles were left to suffer the night in grim circumstances— but not for long.

Deep in the night they woke up to find an angel of God standing right there in the cell with them. To their surprise, the heavy door gaped open behind him. As the angel ushered them out of the prison, he gave them an assignment: "Go to the Temple and give the people this message of life!" (Acts 5:20). In other words, they were to go out and keep doing exactly what had gotten them into trouble in the first place.

This instruction from the angel tells us that the main purpose of the apostles' release was not to ensure their personal safety; it was to advance the Kingdom of Christ. God's seeming lack of concern for their immediate welfare did not offend these men, because they were totally sold out to the cause of Christ. Personal safety was not their focus. They knew that God loved them infinitely, but they also knew that their present life was expendable for the sake of the greater life to come.

When morning came, Caiaphas assembled the Sanhedrin and sent for the prisoners to be brought in. Moments later, the police captain returned, utterly baffled. The prisoners weren't with him. Caiaphas demanded an explanation.

Scripture doesn't go into detail about the captain's reaction, other than to say he was perplexed, but I imagine him nervously clearing his throat and muttering, "Well . . . uh . . . you aren't going to believe this, but when we got to the prison, everything looked completely normal. The guards were standing alert at their posts, and the prison doors were securely locked. But when we opened the doors, the disciples were nowhere to be seen. All the other prisoners are still locked up. Neither they nor the guards saw or heard anything out of the ordinary. There is no evidence of foul play and no damage to the door. It's as if these men vanished into thin air."

As the captain and the leading priests stood around wondering what had happened, a messenger rushed into the chamber and cried, "The men you put in jail are standing in the Temple, teaching the people!" (Acts 5:25).

Impossible! The Sanhedrin's confusion morphed into anger. Not

PETER AND JOHN IN PRISON

The apostles were thrown into a "common" prison, which indicates that this was not what is sometimes called a "courteous" prison, reserved for political prisoners or elite offenders. These cells were filled with the vilest and most ruthless felons. The Sanhedrin members were venting their anger and frustration by treating these persistent thorns in their sides with all the malicious and hostile options they had at their disposal.

only had their prisoners escaped, but they had added insult to injury by going straight back and continuing the very thing they had been arrested for in the first place.

In spite of another undeniable miracle, the Sanhedrin remained single-minded in their focus. Those upstart street preachers had to be silenced. Caiaphas demanded that Peter and John be brought before the council again.

The captain and the Temple guards "arrested the apostles, but without violence, for they were afraid the people would stone them" (Acts 5:26). The captain was obviously intimidated. The people knew that the apostles hadn't broken any laws, and he feared what they might do if he mistreated their heroes. Not only that, but he was shaken by what had happened in his prison the night before. These men had power!

So this time his approach was neither violent nor rough. It was more along these lines: "Uh, gentlemen, would you allow us the honor of escorting you as guests to the Sanhedrin?"

The apostles didn't mind at all. They would get another chance to preach to the leaders of the Jews.

As the apostles stood before the Sanhedrin, Caiaphas confronted them: "We gave you strict orders never again to teach in this man's name! . . . Instead, you have filled all Jerusalem with your teaching about him, and you want to make us responsible for his death!" (Acts 5:28).

Caiaphas's statement leveled three charges at the apostles. The first was insubordination: they had disobeyed the council's order to stop preaching in the name of Jesus. The second charge was indoctrination of the people: the apostles were filling Jerusalem with the doctrine of Jesus' resurrection. And the third charge was incrimination of the Sanhedrin: the apostles were making these Jewish leaders look guilty for murdering the nation's Messiah.

The apostles answered the first two charges with a single statement: "We must obey God rather than any human authority" (Acts 5:29). This was the same answer they'd given when they were arrested before. They were saying, "We cannot help but go on teaching the resurrection of Jesus because it is true, and God has charged us to teach it."

As for the third charge—holding the Sanhedrin responsible for murdering Christ—it seems that the council had conveniently forgotten what they'd said when they brought Jesus to Pilate: "We will take responsibility for his death—we and our children!" (Matthew 27:25). But the apostles didn't back down one inch. In fact, they reiterated their accusation: "The God of our ancestors raised Jesus from the dead after you killed him by hanging him on a cross" (Acts 5:30). Then they took things a step further, asserting that this Christ, whom the Jewish leaders killed, now sits at the right hand of God. He has the power to crush all his enemies, and that, they told the council, includes you. The apostles had turned the tables. It was not they who were on trial; it was the Sanhedrin.

But the apostles didn't stop with the bad news. They followed their accusation with the good news of the gospel. They told the council that this same Christ they'd crucified offered them forgiveness of their sins (Acts 5:31). They were guilty, but there was a way out. If they repented and accepted this generous offer extended by the very man they'd murdered, he would save them. What grace!

But did these men consider the offer? Not for a moment. Their response was automatic: "When they heard this, the high council was furious and decided to kill them" (Acts 5:33). They had abandoned all reason; no amount of truth or evidence would sway them. Their precious doctrine had been utterly shattered, yet they were determined to protect it at any cost. They could not shut these apostles up, so they would shut them down. Their deaths would anger many people, but they figured the furor would die in time. If they allowed these men to keep on preaching, it would be the death of the Sanhedrin's influence, control, and entire belief system.

A Lone Voice of Reason

The Sanhedrin's decision was made: the apostles would be stoned to death. But before Caiaphas could bang the gavel, an aged but venerable figure rose to speak. Everyone paused to listen, for the speaker was the famous and highly respected teacher Gamaliel. Gamaliel urged the council to cool down and think things through before taking a rash action they might later regret. It wasn't what the council wanted to hear, but this was the great Gamaliel, and the least they could do was give him due honor by listening.

Gamaliel briefly recounted two incidents his colleagues would have remembered. Two other men in the recent past had made elaborate claims about themselves and gained surprisingly large followings. While these men were active, they caused alarm for the Sanhedrin, just as Jesus' apostles were doing now. In both cases, however, when the leaders were killed, their followers scattered, and the movements they'd led had died.

Using these incidents as cases in point, Gamaliel gave the Sanhedrin his counsel: "Leave these men alone. Let them go. If they are planning and doing these things merely on their own, it will soon be overthrown.

But if it is from God, you will not be able to overthrow them. You may even find yourselves fighting against God!" (Acts 5:38-39).

Gamaliel's "wait and see" advice allowed for the possibility that the resurrection of Jesus might be true. He may not have been fully convinced, but he had seen the miracles of the apostles, and he understood that the leaders should remain open to the power that might be behind them.

The Reluctant Release

Gamaliel's speech cooled the heads of the Sanhedrin members and reminded them of their precarious standing with the people. Killing the apostles would certainly incite anger, which might lead to serious trouble for the leaders. As much as they hated to do it, they'd be better off letting these troublesome Jesus followers go free.

Yet they had to have their pound of flesh. They ordered severe beatings for Peter and John. And then, hoping this harsh punishment

GAMALIEL

Gamaliel the Elder was a well-known, respected teacher of the law. Though he was a member of the Pharisees, he served on the Sanhedrin, which was composed largely of Sadducees. Gamaliel differed from his fellow Pharisees in that he embraced a more compassionate interpretation of the Jewish law. He held that Sabbath laws, rigorously enforced by the Pharisees, should be interpreted more leniently and realistically, that Jews should be kind to Gentiles, and that the law should be more protective of women. He was also a teacher of Saul, who later became the apostle Paul. Saul's early career of persecuting Christians indicates that Gamaliel's teachings on patience and kindness did not immediately sink in with the young firebrand. Gamaliel died around A.D. 52.

would cool their fervor, the Sanhedrin again warned the apostles not to speak in the name of Jesus.

The natural response for most people when treated as unjustly as these apostles would be outrage. They had done nothing wrong— in fact, they'd merely helped a man in need and spoken life-giving words of truth. Yet they suffered public disgrace, imprisonment, and brutality. But instead of complaining, "the apostles left the high council rejoicing that God had counted them worthy to suffer disgrace for the name of Jesus" (Acts 5:41). Furthermore, they did not back down from their commitment to Jesus even one iota. They immediately returned to their work, teaching the good news of Jesus Christ both publicly in the Temple and privately in homes throughout Jerusalem.

✝ ✝ ✝

The Seriousness of Sin and the Joy of Suffering

Ecclesiastes 10:1 says, "As dead flies cause even a bottle of perfume to stink, so a little foolishness spoils great wisdom and honor." It is from this verse that we get our expression "a fly in the ointment," an appropriate description of the story of Ananias and Sapphira. Because of their greed and deception, the beautiful aroma of the early church was spoiled by the foul smell of sin. The sin may have seemed hidden, but it was not hidden to God. The punishment was severe—a demonstration of God's displeasure with insincerity and its threat to the life of the church. When deception moves into the church, God moves out.

Lessons from a Dramatic Story

Yes, the story of Ananias and Sapphira is dramatic and shocking. But if we focus only on the events and miss the lessons, we will fail to learn what the early church can teach us about following God today.

THE STRATEGY OF SATAN

The Bible says that Satan uses a variety of schemes in his attacks against the people of God (2 Corinthians 2:11; Ephesians 6:11). However, as the "father of lies," Satan has a number-one strategy: deception. Bible scholar John Phillips says, "Deception was at the root of Ananias's sin. The idiom of Satan's language is the lie, deception his stock in trade. This first attack on the church from within was in keeping with his character and his method."[1]

We should not be so naive as to think that Satan no longer strategizes against God's people. He still plots to destroy the work of God by dividing, disgracing, discouraging, and destroying the church. When the church was near its inception, Satan tried to destroy it through the Sanhedrin, and he failed. Then he tried to disgrace the church through Ananias and Sapphira, and he failed. In both cases, the church continued to grow. But Satan won't stop trying. We must remain vigilant and alert against his deceptive and destructive strategies (1 Peter 5:8).

THE SERIOUSNESS OF SIN

When Ananias tried to deceive the church, the apostle Peter reproved him, saying, "You weren't lying to us but to God!" (Acts 5:4). The fact is, all sin is ultimately against God, and that is why it is so serious. John Phillips explains, "Sin is always serious. However, its seriousness is always in proportion to the dignity of the person against whom the sin is committed. It is a serious matter to tell a lie; it is more serious to tell a lie to a judge; it is serious beyond words to lie to God."[2] Pastor and author Colin Smith provides us with a modern-day illustration to help us understand this truth:

> Suppose a middle school student punches another student in class. What happens? The student is given a detention. Suppose during the detention, this boy punches the teacher. What happens? The student gets suspended from school.

Suppose on the way home, the same boy punches a policeman on the nose. What happens? He finds himself in jail. Suppose some years later, the very same boy is in a crowd waiting to see the President of the United States. As the President passes by, the boy lunges forward to punch the President. What happens? He is shot dead by the secret service.[3]

Over the years, many people have asked me if God's judgment of Ananias and Sapphira was too extreme. I like to answer, "Not in the grand scope of Scripture, if we understand the glory of God and the nature of sin." God's judgment against Ananias and Sapphira should be taken for what it is: a reminder that God hates sin and is exceedingly merciful to us when he overlooks our transgressions.

The great preacher Donald G. Barnhouse suggests another reason why this punishment was so severe. The church was just beginning, and in those infant stages it was necessary to firmly establish God's standard of holiness and purity. This couple's sin was like a cancer in the newborn church. If not dealt with, it would spread. Immediate surgery was required to preserve the church's health and vitality. The deaths of Ananias and Sapphira were pointed reminders to the young church that God takes sin seriously—and that its members must take their commitment to him seriously too.

Rejoicing in Suffering

When the council released Peter and John, these two men had been through an ordeal. They'd been arrested and had spent a night in a horrible prison. Then they'd been set free, arrested again, interrogated, and severely beaten. Yet after all that, they "left the high council rejoicing that God had counted them worthy to suffer disgrace for the name of Jesus" (Acts 5:41).

How could anyone want to be worthy of suffering, as if it were a reward for achievement? In and of itself, suffering is not a good thing. It was not a part of God's original intent for human beings. He created the world free of pain, sickness, strife, and conflict. The apostles were not rejoicing in the suffering itself; instead, they were rejoicing in what their suffering meant. They knew that the truth they preached ran counter to the prevailing beliefs and opinions in Jerusalem. So when they encountered suffering as a result of their preaching, it was a sure sign that they were doing something right. They were encountering the natural resistance of a fallen world to a godly message, and the resulting suffering was a medal of honor for persisting in proclaiming it. Through their suffering, they heard God's affirmation to them: "Well done."

We can rejoice in suffering because it proves the authenticity of our faith. The New Testament provides us with at least four other reasons why we can approach the trials of life with joy in our hearts.

SUFFERING PRODUCES GROWTH IN OUR LIVES

The Bible says that when we suffer for righteousness, we experience growth. The best lessons are the ones we learn in hard times. Most of us really don't learn well from prosperity and good times. Paul writes, "We can rejoice, too, when we run into problems and trials, for we know that they help us develop endurance. And endurance develops strength of character, and character strengthens our confident hope of salvation. And this hope will not lead to disappointment. For we know how dearly God loves us, because he has given us the Holy Spirit to fill our hearts with his love" (Romans 5:3-5). James's words echo that truth from Romans: "Dear brothers and sisters, when troubles of any kind come your way, consider it an opportunity for great joy. For you know that when your faith is tested, your endurance has a chance to grow" (James 1:2-3).

James is not saying we are to rejoice about the pain itself; we are to rejoice because God's purposes are being accomplished in our lives. We must learn to look at our difficulties from God's perspective and recognize that, though the trial is not a happy experience in itself, it is God's way of producing something of great value in us.

SUFFERING PROVIDES OPPORTUNITIES TO WITNESS

When the apostle Paul was in prison for speaking boldly about Christ, he wrote, "I want you to know, my dear brothers and sisters, that everything that has happened to me here has helped to spread the Good News. For everyone here, including the whole palace guard, knows that I am in chains because of Christ" (Philippians 1:12-13).

When people suffer for the sake of the gospel, it's often a catalyst to bring others to Christ. Musician Michael Card tells the story of a Muslim man named Joseph who was won to Christ. He was so excited about his new relationship with God that he began proclaiming Christ in his village. He was severely beaten by his neighbors and left for dead outside the village. He returned a few days later thinking he had confused the gospel message somehow, and he began to preach again. For a second time he was beaten and left for dead outside his village. Upon recovering several days later, he again entered the village but was attacked before he could even speak. When he regained consciousness after the third beating, he discovered he was in his own bed, being tended to by the women of his village. The people were so convicted by his courage and willingness to suffer that the entire village turned to Christ.[4]

SUFFERING PROVOKES COURAGE IN OTHERS

Paul's imprisonment had a powerful effect on his friends, inspiring many of them to preach the gospel with great courage: "Because of my imprisonment, most of the believers here have gained confidence and boldly speak God's message without fear" (Philippians 1:14).

Billy Graham is reported to have said, "Courage is contagious. When a brave man takes a stand, the spines of others are often stiffened." Isn't that true? When we see others act with boldness, we are often emboldened ourselves. And when others witness courage in us, some of that bravery may transfer to them as well.

In his book *Let the Nations Be Glad!* author John Piper tells the story of a modern-day missionary whose courage in the midst of suffering inspired countless others to follow his example:

> The execution of Wycliffe missionary Chet Bitterman by the Colombian guerrilla group M-19 on March 6, 1981, unleashed an amazing zeal for the cause of Christ. Chet had been in captivity for seven weeks while his wife, Brenda, and little daughters, Anna and Esther, waited in Bogotá. The demand of M-19 was that Wycliffe get out of Colombia.
>
> They shot him just before dawn—a single bullet to the chest. Police found his body in the bus where he died, in a parking lot in the south of town. He was clean and shaven, his face relaxed. A guerrilla banner wrapped his remains. There were no signs of torture.
>
> In the year following Chet's death, "applications for overseas service with Wycliffe Bible Translators doubled." . . . It is not the kind of missionary mobilization that any of us would choose. But it is God's way. "Unless a grain of wheat falls into the earth and dies, it remains alone; but if it dies, it bears much fruit" (John 12:24).[5]

SUFFERING PREPARES US TO REIGN WITH CHRIST

Jesus tells us to rejoice in persecution because "a great reward awaits you in heaven" (Matthew 5:11-12). Paul says that the suffering must come before the glory: "Together with Christ we are heirs of God's glory. But if we are to share his glory, we must also share his suffering" (Romans 8:17). To suffer persecution is to be an eventual partaker of joy.

Paul told Timothy, "If we endure hardship, we will reign with him" (2 Timothy 2:12). With these words, Paul was reminding his young protégé that suffering precedes—and produces—greater responsibilities. If in the process of being a Christ follower you find yourself facing persecution, remember that you can rejoice because you are being prepared for something greater—heaven!

CHAPTER 6

THE DEATH OF A SERVANT

✝ ✝ ✝

The Story of the
First Christian Martyr

Acts 6–8:4

THE CHURCH IN JERUSALEM was growing beyond the apostles' highest hopes, and it was clear that the Holy Spirit was at work. There was just one problem: the apostles were tired, and they were growing more exhausted every day. When the group of believers was small, the twelve apostles had no problem managing the responsibilities of the early church. But as the number of believers grew, so did the demands on the apostles' time.

Jesus had charged them with preaching the good news of the gospel, beginning in Jerusalem and then throughout the world. But lately they had managed to preach very little, even in Jerusalem. One need after another kept them running—helping a new family find shelter, arbitrating a quarrel between the Asian and Alexandrian converts, overseeing the collection and distribution of donations. Such explosive growth was a wonderful problem to have, but it was still a problem.

To top it off, a disagreement had arisen between the Hebrew

Christians and the Greek-speaking converts. The Greeks claimed that the Hebrews were ignoring their widows in the daily distribution of food (Acts 6:1). Aggravating the complaint was a cultural divide between the two groups. The Hebrew believers spoke Aramaic and read Scripture in Hebrew, while the other group spoke Greek and read the Greek translation. There also may have been a touch of condescension on the part of the Hebrew faction, which grated against the Greek minority.

The conflict between the two sectors was the tipping point for the apostles. They had to find a solution to this growing burden of administration. Their solution was identical to the advice Moses had received from his father-in-law, Jethro, fourteen centuries earlier: it was time to delegate.

The apostles called the multitude of believers together and said, "We apostles should spend our time teaching the word of God, not running a food program. And so, brothers, select seven men who are well respected and are full of the Spirit and wisdom. We will give them this responsibility. Then we apostles can spend our time in prayer and teaching the word" (Acts 6:2-4). The believers chose Stephen, Philip, Prochorus, Nicanor, Timon, Parmenas, and Nicolas. Once the selections were made, the apostles laid their hands on these men and prayed for them, and then they began their work.

Judging by their names, all these men were likely Greeks. Since they were the ones who felt that their people were being slighted, the choice of Greek believers to solve the problem was an exhibition of humility on the part of the Hebrew majority. Two of these men become prominent players in the book of Acts: Philip, whom we will meet in the next chapter, and Stephen, who became known for much more than distributing food.

Stephen under Fire

Stephen was more than a mere table server. Though he willingly performed this task, he had much broader and far-ranging talents

WHAT IS A DEACON?

The New Testament designates only two official offices for the Christian church. The first is elder, also called pastor, bishop, or shepherd. The second is deacon. This office originated in the church in Jerusalem in Acts 6 and was made a formal position as the church grew. Specific qualifications for deacons are given in 1 Timothy 3.

and abilities. He was "a man full of God's grace and power," and he "performed amazing miracles and signs among the people" (Acts 6:8). He and his fellow deacon Philip were the only non-apostles in the New Testament who were said to have performed miracles. As a deacon who cared for sick and suffering believers, Stephen likely performed miracles of healing among them.

Among Stephen's talents was public teaching, and he was quite effective at it. In a sense, one might say that he was too effective for his own good. His preaching soon drew opposition from a group of Jews from the Synagogue of the Freed Slaves. It seems that these Jewish leaders, fearing that Stephen's powerful message of Christ would undermine their religion, challenged him to a formal debate.

That was their big mistake. They quickly found that they were no match for Stephen. Not only did he know his own subject inside and out, but his knowledge of Jewish history and religion matched their own. He was able to turn every argument against Christ back at them by showing how Judaism was meant to pave the way for Christ's arrival.

Stephen's logic was irrefutable, and "none of them could stand against the wisdom and the Spirit with which Stephen spoke"

(Acts 6:10). They were angry; he was winsome. They were loud and abrasive; he was calm. They were insulting; he was respectful. Stephen's attitude probably added fuel to his antagonists' fire. Defeat is hard to take at the hands of someone who is full of joy.

Then these synagogue leaders did what many people do when they lose a debate. Unable to win on the merits of their own arguments, they resorted to deception. They launched a smear campaign against Stephen, misrepresenting and twisting his words. They found people who were willing to spread lies about Stephen and induced them, probably with money, to say, "We heard him blaspheme Moses, and even God" (Acts 6:11).

Their scheme worked. The rumors roiled throughout the city until the Jewish people, elders, and teachers of religious law were up in arms, outraged that another Jesus follower was out to destroy their religion.

Stephen had to be stopped. The leaders seized him and dragged him before Caiaphas and the Sanhedrin. They already had false witnesses lined up to spin Stephen's words in ways that were certain to

JEWISH SYNAGOGUES

When the Temple was destroyed, the exiled Jews in Babylon began to worship in local gatherings called synagogues. At these assemblies, people read Scripture and heard teaching about it. The synagogues also served as public meeting places—much like town halls or public squares. During Stephen's time, Jerusalem had as many as 480 synagogues. The Synagogue of Freed Slaves, which is mentioned in Acts 6, was composed largely of Jews who had once been slaves in Rome, Cyrene, Alexandria, Cilicia, and Roman provinces in Asia Minor.

enrage the council. After this parade of lies, they accused Stephen of four counts of blasphemy. First, the synagogue leaders said, he had blasphemed Moses and God. Second, he had blasphemed the Temple, saying that Jesus would someday destroy it. Third, he had blasphemed the law. And finally, he had blasphemed the Jewish religion by claiming that Jesus would undermine the rituals they'd followed for centuries.

The council turned to Stephen for his response. No doubt they expected him to look terrified. These were serious charges; blasphemy was, in fact, a capital offense according to Jewish law. But as they glared at him, his face took on the aura of an angel (Acts 6:15).

What could this mean? It's not likely that his face looked anything like the angels we see on greeting cards and paintings—soft, effeminate beings looking up rapturously, hands folded in ethereal devotion. Whenever angels appear to people in the Bible, the first thing they say is "Do not be afraid." Why do they say this? Apparently because seeing an angel is a terrifying experience. Angels often appear as bright as lightning and powerful enough to destroy cities. No doubt the angelic look on Stephen's face was one of boldness, power, confidence, certainty, and intelligence. Or it's possible that his face actually shone like Moses' face did after his forty days on a mountain in the presence of God (Exodus 34:29).

No doubt Stephen's refusal to be intimidated frustrated Caiaphas and the council beyond endurance. *What is it about these people?* they must have thought. This was the fourth time individuals from this troublesome movement had been brought before them. They had once faced Jesus himself, his disciples Peter and John twice, and now this man Stephen. Every one of them had been calm, confident, and utterly unafraid. It was infuriating.

"Are these accusations true?" Caiaphas asked.

Without hesitation, Stephen stepped up and launched into his brilliant defense.

Stephen on Trial

"Brothers and fathers, listen to me," Stephen began. "Our glorious God appeared to our ancestor Abraham in Mesopotamia before he settled in Haran" (Acts 7:2).

Caiaphas and the council must have rolled their eyes. Yet another Jesus follower (and a Greek, at that) was about to try to give them, the scholars and teachers of the law, a lesson in Jewish history. They had already heard it twice from Peter and John, the fishermen. But as they were about to see, Stephen's address was more than just a recounting of Israel's history. It was a direct and eloquent answer to each of the accusations against him.

To answer the first charge that he had blasphemed Moses and God, Stephen began telling the story of Israel's great patriarchs—from Abraham, whom God had made the father of their nation, to Moses, through whom God had led the Israelites out of slavery in Egypt. Stephen told of God feeding the Israelites in the wilderness and giving them the law, enabling them to know his will.

Far from dishonoring God or Moses, Stephen affirmed God's faithfulness to Abraham and to his special people. In essence, he was saying, "How can you possibly accuse me of blaspheming God when I honor him as the founder and sustainer of our entire nation?"

Next, Stephen defended himself against the charge of blaspheming against the law. He noted that it was Moses who received the law from God on Mount Sinai and passed it on to the people. With this statement, Stephen affirmed his honor of Moses and acknowledged God as the ultimate lawgiver. He further demonstrated his respect for the law by referring to it as "life-giving words" (Acts 7:38).

Then Stephen turned the tables on the council and showed them that Israel's entire history, from Moses on, had been a sordid one of increasing disrespect for God's law. God repeatedly sent prophets to warn the Israelites that their disobedience would lead to destruction. As an example, he quoted the prophet Amos: "'Was it to me you were bringing sacrifices and offerings during those forty years in the wilderness, Israel? No, you carried your pagan gods—the shrine of Molech, the star of your god Rephan, and the images you made to worship them. So I will send you into exile as far away as Babylon.'" (Acts 7:42-43).

Stephen insisted that he had never spoken against the law. He had merely followed the lead of the prophets and had spoken about the consequences for those who failed to follow it. These leaders of the Jewish nation were the ones blaspheming the law, because they refused to believe in Christ, whom their entire Scriptures predicted.

In defending himself against the charge of blaspheming the Jewish Temple, Stephen gave a brief history of the Temple, beginning with its forerunner—the portable place of worship known as the Tabernacle—and ending with Solomon's permanent Temple in Jerusalem.

Then Stephen boldly accused the council of distorting the purpose of the Temple. They thought God dwelled only within the Temple and nowhere else. But this thinking once again demonstrated their disregard for their own Scriptures. Stephen quoted Isaiah, capturing God's words:

"Heaven is my throne,
    and the earth is my footstool.
Could you build me a temple as good as that?"
    asks the LORD.
"Could you build me such a resting place?
    Didn't my hands make both heaven and earth?"
ACTS 7:49-50

These Jewish leaders had ignored Isaiah's words and elevated their Temple to the point of diminishing God. Talk about blasphemy! It didn't get much worse than thinking they could confine the God who created the universe to a building of their own making.

Stephen's defense against the first three charges was so thorough that he didn't bother to address the fourth charge of undermining Jewish traditions. His entire survey of Israel's history showed his deep respect for all the traditions of Israel—God, Moses, the law, and the Temple.

Stephen had finished his defense, but he had one further message to deliver. It wasn't a message these leaders wanted to hear, but Stephen was willing to deliver it, regardless of the consequences. He turned to the Jewish leaders and leveled a deadly charge at them: "You stubborn people! You are heathen at heart and deaf to the truth. Must you forever resist the Holy Spirit?" (Acts 7:51).

No doubt Stephen knew he would never get out of their clutches alive, and he was determined that he would draw his last breath delivering God's truth. He told them that they were just like their ancestors, who had repeatedly flouted God's law. "Name one prophet your ancestors didn't persecute!" he cried. "They even killed the ones who predicted the coming of the Righteous One—the Messiah whom you betrayed and murdered. You deliberately disobeyed God's law, even though you received it from the hands of angels" (Acts 7:52-53).

The implication of Stephen's words was crystal clear to these men. Stephen had turned the tables. He was accusing them of being the ones who had blasphemed God, Moses, the law, and the Temple by rejecting the Messiah—the one all the Old Testament Scriptures and Jewish traditions pointed to.

Stephen's Unjust Verdict

When the Sanhedrin responded to Stephen's charge, it lashed out like a wounded animal. The council members didn't ask questions for clarification. They didn't try to refute any of Stephen's points or counter his claims. They didn't pause to deliberate or confer among themselves. They didn't even follow the procedure of formally pronouncing judgment. Instead, these dignified Jewish leaders "were infuriated by Stephen's accusation, and they shook their fists at him in rage" (Acts 7:54).

As he watched these supposedly sane men lose control of themselves, Stephen knew that he was in the last moments of his life. Then God, in his love and grace, granted this courageous man a heavenly vision. Stephen looked up and shouted, "Look, I see the heavens opened and the Son of Man standing in the place of honor at God's right hand!" (Acts 7:56).

That's when any vestiges of sanity among the Jewish leaders disappeared. They clapped their hands over their ears, growling like ravenous animals to drown out Stephen's voice. They knew that when Stephen said that Christ was seated at the right hand of God, he was claiming that Christ was equal with God. They couldn't stand to hear this. "They rushed at him and dragged him out of the city and began to stone him" (Acts 7:57-58).

The word *rushed* in this passage is translated from the same Greek word used to describe the demon-possessed pigs that plunged to their death in Matthew 8:32. One man's truthful preaching reduced Israel's highest court to a depraved mob of frothing beasts.

They dragged Stephen from the council chamber and took him outside the city to stone him. There was a rigidly prescribed procedure for stoning an offender, but in their madness, these meticulous keepers of the law ignored all protocol. They tore off their coats, scooped up large rocks, and began to hurl them at this man whom they couldn't silence any other way.

With stones bruising his head and limbs, lacerating his skin, and shattering his ribs and bones, Stephen managed to remain standing until he had prayed, "Lord Jesus, receive my spirit" (Acts 7:59). Finally, unable to stand, Stephen sank to his knees and shouted his last words: "Lord, don't charge them with this sin!" (Acts 7:60). Then he collapsed in a bloody heap and died.

When the panting Jewish leaders finally dropped their stones and walked away, devout men from the church came and buried Stephen's body. The church mourned greatly over the loss of one of their finest.

The Multiplication Continues

The resentment against the church stirred up by the synagogue leaders didn't fade with Stephen's death. Rumors continued to buzz that the Jesus movement was out to undermine the Jewish faith and destroy the Temple. The leaders had eliminated one of the movement's most effective spokesmen, but that only egged them on to go after the others as well. They made it their mission to destroy this burgeoning church and forever end its threat to their comfortable way of life.

As a result of the massive persecution, believers began to flee for their lives and relocate to other cities throughout Judea and Samaria. The apostles remained in Jerusalem to weather the storm and maintain a stable center for the spreading church.

No doubt the Jewish leaders were delighted with the flight of the believers. Surely their city would soon be cleansed of this spreading

DEATH BY STONING

Stoning was the punishment prescribed in the Old Testament for capital sins, including idolatry, witchcraft, and blasphemy (Leviticus 20:2, 27; 24:14, 16). Stoning involved a three-step process. First, the offender—with his hands and feet bound—was pushed off a high pedestal onto stony ground. Often the fall would break his skull, killing him. If it didn't, the second step would be implemented: the offender would be turned onto his back and a large boulder would be dropped on his chest. This would crush his ribs and his vital organs. If that failed, the stoning went to the third step: the entire crowd gathered around would hurl stones at the offender until he was dead.

cancer. But their efforts had an effect they didn't anticipate: the scattering believers "preached the Good News about Jesus wherever they went" (Acts 8:4). By the Jewish leaders' calculations, they were going to subtract from the church. But God had other plans: he was multiplying it.

+ + +

The Glory of Being a Servant

Peggy Noonan was a speechwriter for former president Ronald Reagan. As someone who had regular contact with the president, she was constantly asked about the kind of man he was. In these situations, she would often tell the "bathroom story," which went like this:

> A few days after President Reagan was shot, when he was well enough to get out of bed, he went into the bathroom that connected to his room and slapped some water on his face to wake himself up. In the process, he spilled some water out of the basin and all over the floor. So he got some paper towels and knelt down on the floor to clean it up.
>
> An aide went to check on the President and there he was, on the floor with paper towels, cleaning up the water that had spilled out of the basin. The aide said to him, "Mr. President, what are you doing? Let the nurse clean that up."
>
> But he said, "Oh, no. I made that mess, and I'd hate for the nurse to have to clean it up."

Ronald Reagan was the most powerful leader in the world, yet he was marked by a surprising humility of character. In Noonan's mind, President Reagan was great because he would rather serve than be served.[1]

The Greatness of Serving

The book of Acts tells us about the church's first deacons—men chosen to distribute food to those in need. The Bible tells us that these servants were necessary so the apostles could continue the work Christ had specifically trained them to do, which was preaching and teaching.

The typical view of organizational hierarchy can lead us to interpret this incident the wrong way, as if the apostles were saying, "Our position is too lofty to stoop to such menial tasks. We need underlings to do these jobs." That wasn't their attitude at all, as we can see by the fact that they had been serving the needy themselves until the burden interfered with their primary calling.

There was a time when these apostles had seen things quite differently. When they assembled in the upper room for their last Passover meal with Jesus, they hadn't hired any servants to wash their feet. They wore sandals and traveled by walking, which meant their feet quickly became caked with dust. No one was willing to perform the lowly foot-washing task for the others. Why should they grovel on their knees like a common housemaid?

Then Jesus himself turned all ideas of servanthood completely upside down for them—and for us—when he filled a basin with water, got down on his knees, and washed the filthy feet of his disciples. Can you imagine? Here was God himself, who had come to save the entire world, washing the feet of sinners he had come to save.

Here Jesus illustrated a principle he had shared with his disciples after one of their disputes: "Whoever wants to be a leader among you must be your servant, and whoever wants to be first among you must become your slave. For even the Son of Man came not to be served but to serve others and to give his life as a ransom for many" (Matthew 20:26-28).

Both the apostles and Stephen understood this principle. That's why Stephen, with his many talents, was willing to serve anywhere he was needed, whether it was the menial work of handing out food or the dangerous work of spreading the gospel of Christ. In his service and in his death, he was a shining example of selflessness and servanthood.

Dwight L. Moody once said, "The measure of a man is not how many servants he has, but how many men he serves." And Moody was a man whose life matched his words. In his book *A Call to Excellence*, Gary Inrig tells this story:

> A large group of European pastors came to one of D. L. Moody's Bible Conferences in the late 1800s. Following the European custom of the time, each guest put his shoes outside his room to be cleaned by the hall servants overnight. But of course this was America, and there were no hall servants.
>
> Walking the dormitory halls that night, Moody saw the shoes and determined not to embarrass his brothers. He mentioned the need to some ministerial students who were there, but was met with only silence or pious excuses. So Moody returned to the dorm, gathered up the shoes, and, alone in his room, the world's most famous evangelist began to clean and polish the shoes. Only the unexpected arrival of a friend in the midst of the work revealed the secret.
>
> When the foreign visitors opened their doors the next morning, their shoes were shined. They never knew by whom. Moody told no one, but his friend told a few people, and during the rest of the conference, different men volunteered to shine the shoes in secret. Perhaps the episode is a vital insight into why God used D. L. Moody as He did. He was a man with a servant's heart and that was the basis of his true greatness.[2]

Few of us will have the impact of Ronald Reagan or D. L. Moody, but we all have the potential to be great. In the words of Martin Luther

King Jr., "Everybody can be great because anybody can serve. You don't have to have a college degree to serve. You don't have to make your subject and verb agree to serve. You don't have to know Plato and Aristotle. You don't have to know Einstein's theory of relativity. You don't have to know the second theory of thermodynamics in physics. You only need a heart full of grace. A soul generated by love."[3]

The Challenge of Serving

Most of us won't die the death of a martyr, but Jesus still calls us to die to ourselves and serve one another in practical, and often mundane, ways. Author and pastor Calvin Miller accurately describes the challenge of serving others: "Unfortunately, serving people is the only way by which we can serve God. And serving people means that we're going to get hurt in the process. And if we're not careful, the pain involved in our service can cause us to ultimately despise those we once felt called to love. Charlie Brown is right: we all want to serve God, but it can be terribly degrading to serve people to do it."[4]

Or, as the old saying goes:

To love the whole world for me is no chore,
My only real problem is the neighbor next door.

Yes, it is often hardest to love those who are closest to us. The busyness of life can make it inconvenient for us to stop and help those who are "in our way." And the more we know someone, the easier it is for us to grow weary or frustrated by what we perceive to be his or her weaknesses or idiosyncrasies.

But when we serve those who are closest to us, we are changing the world. Think how different the world would be if every husband simply served and loved his wife and encouraged and loved his children. Or if every family cared for the neighbor next door. Although it's rarely easy or glamorous, when we love others in humble and ordinary ways, we are making a great impact on the world and reflecting the life of Jesus, who chose to love not from a distance but by coming close to us and loving us when we were unlovable.

Pastor and author Gordon MacDonald tells a wonderful story about the everyday lifestyle of service each one of us can pursue:

[My wife], Gail, and I were in an airplane . . . seated almost at the back. . . . As the plane loaded up, a woman with two small children came down the aisle to take the seat right in front of us. And behind her, another woman. The two women took the A and C seats, and one of the children sat in the middle seat, and the second child was on the lap of one of the women. I figured these were two mothers traveling together with their kids, and I hoped the kids wouldn't be noisy.

The flight started, and my prayer wasn't answered. The two children had a tough time. The air was turbulent, the children cried a lot—their ears hurt—and it was a miserable flight. I watched as these two women kept trying to help and comfort these children. The woman at the window played with the child in the middle seat, trying to make her feel good and paying lots of attention.

I thought, *These women get a medal for what they are doing.* But things went downhill from there. As we got towards the last part of the flight, the child in the middle seat got sick. The next thing I knew she was losing everything from every part of her body. . . . Before long a stench began to rise through the cabin. It was unbearable!

I could see over the top of the seat that indescribable stuff was all over everything. It was on this woman's clothes. It was all over the seat. It was on the floor. It was one of the most repugnant things I had seen in a long time.

I watched as the woman next to the window patiently comforted the child and tried her best to clean up the mess and make something out of a bad situation. The plane landed, and when we pulled up to the gate all of us were ready to exit that plane as fast as we could. The flight attendant came up with paper towels and handed them to the woman in the window seat and said, "Here, Ma'am, these are for your little girl."

The woman said, "This isn't my little girl."

"Aren't you traveling together?"

"No, I've never met this woman and these children before in my life."

Suddenly I realized this woman had just been merciful. . . . She had found the opportunity to give mercy. She was, in the words of Christ, "the person who was the neighbor."[5]

The Reward of Serving

The great nineteenth-century Hungarian composer Franz Liszt wrote a moving symphonic poem entitled "Les Préludes." This is how he described the meaning of the piece, as inscribed on the original musical score: "What else is our life but a series of preludes to that unknown Hymn, the first and solemn note of which is intoned by Death?" In other words, our present life is merely a prelude, a preparation. We are tuning our instruments and honing our skills to be ready to join the orchestra in that grand hymn of eternal life. Death merely sounds the first note of that symphony.

Stephen's life is a shining example of what Liszt sought to convey in his poem. For Stephen, death was not a horror. Though momentarily painful, it was the first note of his forever. Or, in another metaphor, it was his gateway to the life he had prepared for throughout his service to the church.

Some Bible translations describe the moment of Stephen's death by saying that he "fell asleep." This is a common New Testament term for death. In reality, however, we know that it was only Stephen's body that fell asleep. His heart quit beating, and his lungs ceased breathing. His body would "sleep" in the grave until the final resurrection of all believers. Stephen's soul, on the other hand, did not fall asleep. The core of him remained very much alive as he passed from one dimension of reality into a greater one.

What Stephen saw moments before that transition gives us one of the Bible's most vivid affirmations of the existence of a future life. He looked up to see "the heavens opened and the Son of Man standing in the place of honor at God's right hand!" (Acts 7:56) It may be significant that Stephen saw Christ *standing* at God's right hand. Both Jesus himself and the apostle Paul refer to Christ sitting at God's right hand—an indication of his eternal reign. The fact that Stephen saw him standing may well mean he had risen from his throne to welcome his dear and faithful servant who had held fast to him, even in the face of death.

If we can hold before our eyes the picture of Christ that Stephen saw, there should be no difficulty, no pain, no ridicule, no persecution, no obstacle of any kind that would deter us from being a faithful servant of Christ. May we follow Stephen's example and remain steadfast to Christ regardless of how hot the fire or how heavy the stones might be.

CHAPTER 7

THE TRAVELING PREACHER

✝ ✝ ✝

The Story of the First
Christian Evangelist

Acts 8

AFTER THE DEATH OF STEPHEN, believers scattered from Jerusalem to escape the Jewish leaders' campaign to extinguish the church.

Philip, one of the newly appointed deacons, fled north to Samaria. This was not a desirable destination, as observant Jews went to great lengths to avoid having anything to do with Samaritans. In the first century, Jews had utter disdain for the Samaritans, whom they considered lower-class, half-breed Jews. When traveling between Judea and Galilee, Jews took the long road around Samaria to avoid having contact with Samaritans, even though doing so just about doubled their travel time.

Though Philip was a Jew, he may not have shared this prejudice, having been born in a Greek-speaking country. Even if he had been raised with this bias, however, his new faith opened his heart to love all people, knowing that Jesus died for them as well as for him.

On his arrival in Samaria, Philip didn't remain aloof. He plunged into the culture and proclaimed the message that was now the central passion of his heart. He told these rejected people that the Messiah had come, that he had died and been resurrected, and that he now offered redemption from sin and eternal life. Philip attested to the truth of his message by performing miraculous healings and casting demons out of possessed people.

Philip Encounters the Magician

Living in Samaria at this time was an extraordinary magician named Simon, whose sorcery astonished the citizens of the city. He was highly influential and boasted a huge following. He was also a shameless self-promoter, "claiming to be someone great" (Acts 8:9). His followers swallowed the line, calling him "the Great One—the Power of God" (Acts 8:10). Simon was a dominating presence in Samaria and seemed to have the people eating out of his hand.

Then along came Philip, invading Simon's territory and demonstrating powers of healing and control over demons that Simon could

SAMARIA

Samaria was the name given to both a region and the dominant city within that region. It was located between the Jewish provinces of Galilee to the north and Judea to the south, and it roughly comprised what is now the West Bank in central Israel. Samaria was populated by a group of people who were of mixed descent. Six centuries earlier, when Israel was conquered by Assyria and the rest of the Jews were sent into exile, only the poor were left behind. The Samaritans descended from these Jews who remained and intermarried with the occupying Assyrians, thus corrupting their bloodlines and their religion. Jews despised Samaritans, considering them impure, and avoided all social interactions with them.

not duplicate. His occult magic seemed trivial by comparison. The Samaritans began to drift away from Simon and follow Philip. Not only were they impressed with Philip's miracles, but they were also drawn to his message. These people who were accustomed to being rejected by the Jews were overwhelmed that the Messiah who Israel had been waiting for loved them and desired to include them in his Kingdom. We read that "the people believed Philip's message of Good News concerning the Kingdom of God and the name of Jesus Christ. As a result, many men and women were baptized" (Acts 8:12).

In addition to being successful with magic, Simon was also astute when it came to reading people. Though he was alarmed at Philip's threat to his influence, he knew better than to attack this newcomer whose message and healings had won the hearts of the

THE CHURCH'S VIEW OF WOMEN

According to the Jewish tradition, only males could be ritually initiated into the religion. Women were excluded from full acceptance and participation, both in religious ceremonies and in society. They were separated in synagogues, were barred from testifying in court, didn't have the opportunity to go to school, and could not initiate divorce but could be divorced by their husbands. Women's lives were considered to be of such little value that Lot offered his daughters to the Sodomites to protect his guests (Genesis 19:6-8). A Levite who was threatened by depraved men from the tribe of Benjamin gave them his concubine to protect himself (Judges 19:23-24). Jewish men notoriously prayed, "Lord, thank you for not making me a Gentile, a slave, or a woman." But Acts 8:12 shows that the New Testament church accepted women as equals. The apostle Paul later affirmed this equality, saying that there is no difference in value between male and female, "for you are all one in Christ Jesus" (Galatians 3:28).

people. Furthermore, Simon craved the power he saw Philip wielding, and opposition would certainly prevent him from acquiring it. Therefore, Simon adopted a pragmatic approach: he decided to join forces with Philip. He would begin by becoming an initiate and then work his way into Philip's confidence and acquire the secret to his power.

Acts 8:13 says, "Simon himself believed and was baptized. He began following Philip wherever he went, and he was amazed by the signs and great miracles Philip performed." Notice that Simon exhibited all the signs of someone who has truly repented and converted to Christ: he believed, he was baptized, and he followed. But in his case, the outward signs of a true believer masked a deep deception in his heart. His "conversion" was not about Jesus; it was about Simon. He didn't want repentance; he wanted power. His profession of Christianity was merely a step toward fulfilling his selfish cravings.

The Deceiver Is Exposed

News of Philip's wildly successful evangelistic campaign soon reached the ears of the apostles in Jerusalem. They sent Peter and John to Samaria to see if they could help Philip. On their arrival, they found that although the Samaritans had been baptized in the name of Christ, none of them had received the Holy Spirit.

This may have seemed odd to the apostles. The masses of people who had been baptized on Pentecost had received the Holy Spirit at the time of their conversion, as did subsequent converts in Jerusalem. But they also knew that God in his creativity is not bound to do the same thing in every circumstance, especially when he is looking to meet a particular need.

The evangelization of Samaria was one of those cases. God had temporarily withheld the Holy Spirit from the Samaritans in order to unite them with their Jewish brothers and sisters. So Peter and John, obedient to the will of God, prayed for them to receive the Holy

Spirit and laid hands on them. Then the Holy Spirit came into the lives of these long-shunned people.

When these two apostles—the kind of Jews who traditionally disdained Samaritans—came to Samaria and passed on a precious gift they had received themselves, it signaled the end of the centuries-old rejection the Samaritans had endured and the beginning of a new era of acceptance. Both Jews and Samaritans were now fully embraced as members of God's family—brothers and sisters in Christ.

Simon looked on this imparting of the Holy Spirit with awe. It was a new power, one even greater than Philip had exhibited. He had never seen anything like it, and he wanted to possess it—at any cost. No more subterfuge; no more games. He boldly approached Peter and offered him a sizable price. "Let me have this power, too," he exclaimed, "so that when I lay my hands on people, they will receive the Holy Spirit!" (Acts 8:19).

Peter didn't pull any punches. He delivered a strong rebuke to Simon: "May your money be destroyed with you for thinking God's gift can be bought! You can have no part in this, for your heart is not right with God. Repent of your wickedness and pray to the Lord. Perhaps he will forgive your evil thoughts, for I can see that you are full of bitter jealousy and are held captive by sin" (Acts 8:20-23).

Immediately all Simon's dreams of power and influence collapsed like a sand castle, swept away by a wave of sheer terror. He stood in danger of being condemned by the very power he had craved. "Pray to the Lord for me," he exclaimed, "that these terrible things you've said won't happen to me!" (Acts 8:24).

The Bible doesn't tell us what happened to Simon after this. His agonized plea for Peter's prayers seems motivated by fear, but it also seems heartfelt. Fear is not the best motivator toward God, for its driving force is concern for self rather than love for God. Yet it is a motivator that indicates some level of real belief. It recognizes the reality of God and his power, which may be enough to lead someone to full repentance and real conversion. God uses any method available to turn us toward him. If fear causes us to reach out to him, he can take our hand and pull us up, for he himself is the antidote to fear. "Perfect love expels all fear" (1 John 4:18).

A One-on-One Encounter

Philip's evangelistic campaign in Samaria was a huge success, one that any preacher might envy. People responded in staggering numbers. He proclaimed the truth of Christ in a way that completely shut down an influential leader who easily could have been an obstacle to the believers there. The new church in Samaria was thriving, and the apostles themselves were impressed with all he had done.

At this point—the very pinnacle of Philip's success—an angel appeared to him and told him to pull up stakes and leave the city. "Go south down the desert road that runs from Jerusalem to Gaza" (Acts 8:26).

"What?" Philip could have responded. "You want me to leave what I've built here and go out into a desert filled with lizards and scorpions? I have a following. The church needs me. How can you ask me to give up all I've built and hand it over to those apostles who came in after I did all the work? It's just not fair!"

But Philip said none of this. He didn't ask why; he didn't beg to stay. He just did as he was told. Like his great ancestor Abraham, Philip obeyed and went, not knowing where God would lead him (Hebrews 11:8).

Philip left Samaria and went to Gaza, toward the Mediterranean coast. As he walked along the desert road, he came upon a chariot traveling south from Jerusalem. It was not the two-wheeled war chariot that often appears in period movies; it was a four-wheeled vehicle more like a coach—no doubt an elaborate and well-furnished one. A driver sat in the front, and behind him sat a man who was looking at something and muttering to himself.

The Holy Spirit gave this message to Philip: "Go over and walk along beside the carriage" (Acts 8:29). Philip ran up to the vehicle, and when he approached, he saw that the passenger was reading out loud from a scroll. Philip recognized the words; they were from the prophetic book of Isaiah. He called out to the man, "Do you understand what you are reading?"

The man replied, "How can I, unless someone instructs me?" (Acts 8:30-31).

The man invited Philip into the carriage with him. Philip learned that the man was an Ethiopian eunuch occupying the high position of treasurer under the nation's queen. He was likely a black man who had become a Jewish proselyte, for he had traveled to Jerusalem to worship and was now returning home. No doubt while in Jerusalem he had heard claims that the crucified Jesus was the Messiah prophesied by Isaiah. Scrolls were extremely rare and expensive in that era, but this wealthy eunuch had probably purchased it to learn more about the Messiah.

Eunuchs were often appointed as servants to royalty, and it was not uncommon for talented eunuchs to rise to high positions. But this man's status as a eunuch separated him from his community in significant ways. He was excluded from married love. He was deprived of the joys of family. He was an oddity in society, seen as less of a man. And even though he was a Jewish proselyte, his physical condition would have excluded him from entering the Temple in Jerusalem (Deuteronomy 23:1).

Philip, however, accepted the Ethiopian man fully and was eager to help him understand the prophecy from Isaiah that was confusing him:

> He was led like a sheep to the slaughter.
>> And as a lamb is silent before the shearers,
>> he did not open his mouth.
> He was humiliated and received no justice.
>> Who can speak of his descendants?
>> For his life was taken from the earth.

ACTS 8:32-33

"Tell me," the eunuch said, "was the prophet talking about himself or someone else?" (Acts 8:34).

That was the perfect question to launch Philip into the story of Jesus. The eunuch had been reading the passage in Isaiah that refers to the Messiah as the suffering servant who would be executed like a sheep led to slaughter. Philip no doubt explained that this passage predicted with precise accuracy Jesus' trial before Pilate, his silence in the presence of his accusers, his brutal treatment by the Jewish rulers, and his death on the cross as ransom for the sins of the world.

DO WE STILL NEED THE OLD TESTAMENT?

Some Christians virtually ignore the Old Testament, thinking the New Testament renders it irrelevant. This is a mistake. We learn the human story—who we are and why we need redemption—by reading the Old Testament. The Old Testament reveals the origin of humankind, the nature of sin, the result of disobedience, the character of God, and his unfolding purpose. Perhaps the most obvious benefit is that the Old Testament reveals Christ through hundreds of specific prophecies about his life and death. This is why Philip could teach about Christ from the Old Testament book of Isaiah. As the adage says, "The Old Testament is the New Testament concealed; the New Testament is the Old Testament revealed."

At this point the eunuch may have thought, *Here's a man who was despised and rejected as an outcast, much as I am.* He may have especially identified with the humiliation Jesus faced—particularly the plaintive lament that he would have no descendants. Whatever else he may have thought, we know with certainty that Philip's explanation cleared away the eunuch's confusion and led him to believe that the one Isaiah was speaking of was the one who redeemed him from sin. He responded to Philip's message with complete faith. He was ready to submit his life to the one who had died for him.

Soon Philip and the eunuch came to a small body of water, and the eunuch didn't want to delay his response another minute. He pointed and said, "See, here is water. What hinders me from being baptized?"

"If you believe with all your heart, you may," Philip said.

The eunuch responded with this confession: "I believe that Jesus Christ is the Son of God" (Acts 8:36-37, NKJV).

The eunuch ordered the carriage to be stopped, and Philip took him down into the water to be baptized. When the eunuch came out of the water, he looked around, and Philip was nowhere to be seen. Once his task was successfully completed, the Holy Spirit snatched him away for another mission. The eunuch never saw Philip again. He climbed back into his carriage and continued his journey back to Ethiopia, filled with more joy than he'd ever experienced before. He had been fully accepted into the family of God.

Philip suddenly found himself in the middle of a town called Azotus, formerly the Philistine city Ashdod, which was about thirty miles north of Gaza. He knew why he'd been brought there—to deliver the same Good News he'd been preaching since he left Jerusalem. After spreading the gospel in Azotus, he journeyed north toward Caesarea, stopping to preach in every town along the way.

✝ ✝ ✝

The Good News Is for Everyone

Jesus gave his disciples their marching orders in Acts 1:8: "You will receive power when the Holy Spirit comes upon you. And you will be my witnesses, telling people about me everywhere—in Jerusalem, throughout Judea, in Samaria, and to the ends of the earth." The first seven chapters of Acts give a record of the early church fulfilling the first part of the Lord's instructions. The early believers were indeed witnesses in Jerusalem. In fact, up to this point in the book of Acts, all the events took place in or near Jerusalem.

But in Acts 8, the ministry of the gospel spreads into Judea and Samaria. We read about Philip preaching the gospel in Samaria and about Peter and John giving the gospel "in many Samaritan villages" (Acts 8:25).

The Implications of the Gospel

As the gospel begins to spread outside of Jerusalem, the implications of the Christian message become clear: the gospel is more inclusive, diverse, and personal than anyone could have imagined.

THE GOSPEL IS INCLUSIVE

Today we often hear complaints against Christianity for being too exclusive. "What right do those Christians have to claim that Jesus is the only way to God? Isn't that arrogant and intolerant of other religions?"

Although Christianity is exclusive, it is actually the most inclusive of all religions. Pastor Tim Keller explains:

> The universal religion of humankind is: We develop a good record and give it to God, and then he owes us. The gospel is: God develops a good record and gives it to us, then

we owe him (Rom. 1:17). In short, to say a good person, not just Christians, can find God is to say good works are enough. . . . So the apparently inclusive approach is really quite exclusive. It says, "The good people can find God, and the bad people do not." But what about us moral failures? We are excluded. . . . So both approaches are exclusive, but the gospel's is the more inclusive exclusivity. It says joyfully, "It doesn't matter who you are or what you've done. It doesn't matter if you've been at the gates of hell. You can be welcomed and embraced fully and instantly through Christ."[1]

Jesus is the only way to God. As he himself said, "I am the way, the truth, and the life. No one can come to the Father except through me" (John 14:6). But he invites everyone to come through him. He excludes no one. People can exclude themselves and reject that invitation, but that rejection is not an exclusion imposed by Christianity; it is self-imposed. It's a bit irrational for someone who rejects an invitation to accuse the host of inhospitality.

BAPTISM

The word *baptize* comes from the Greek *baptizó*, which means "to dip or immerse." Immersion into the water provides a vivid picture of what happens in people's souls when they become Christians. They die to their old life ruled by sin and are raised up into a new life ruled by the Holy Spirit. Baptism resembles burial, as the new believer is immersed into the water, and resurrection, as he or she is raised from it. Baptism itself does not impart new life, as there is no mystical power in the water. The Holy Spirit is the one who gives new life. Baptism is an external picture of that internal reality.

Acts 8 makes it clear that no one who wants to come to Christ is excluded. The invitation is offered to everyone. This includes men and women from all ethnicities, all cultures, and all nationalities. The Good News overcomes all prejudices and includes those who have been overlooked or cast aside as unworthy. No one is beyond the reach of the gospel.

A case in point was the magician Simon. We don't know whether Simon was saved. He was offered the chance to repent, even though he had a lot to repent of. He was a prideful man who craved power and soaked up adulation at every opportunity he got. Such pride is reminiscent of Adam's original sin of putting himself above God. Worse, by practicing occult arts, Simon was actively opposing God by consorting with God's adversaries in the spiritual realm. In that time, magicians were not mere stage entertainers who developed illusions to amaze audiences; magicians actually attempted to reach into the spirit world and draw on invisible powers to manipulate elements in the physical world.

Yet in spite of these egregious sins, Peter invited Simon to repent and come into the Kingdom of God. No matter how terrible the sin, God stands ready to forgive and accept those who reject their former lives and commit to a new life in the Holy Spirit.

THE GOSPEL IS DIVERSE

The Jews and the Samaritans had significant cultural differences. They had different versions of Scripture. The Samaritans recognized only the Torah—the first five books of the Old Testament—while the Jews' canon included all the books Protestants today recognize to be the Old Testament. Samaritans worshiped on Mount Gerizim; Jews worshiped in Jerusalem. The two groups had different heritages, which meant that different religious and social practices had been passed down from previous generations. Yet none of these differences stood in the way of their mutual inclusion in the body of Christ.

When Jews and Samaritans turned to Jesus, they found in him the uniting factor that rose above these differences.

First-century Christians differed on which holy days should be celebrated and which foods were forbidden. In the twenty-first century, Christians differ on things like Bible translations, worship styles, and theological nuances such as predestination, eschatology, and modes of baptism. This kind of diversity can be embraced as long as there is unity on the essentials—the central beliefs of Christianity, as embodied in the great creeds developed in the early centuries of the church.[2]

These differences are minor in light of the unity that binds us together in Christ. As the apostle Paul said, "I appeal to you, dear brothers and sisters, by the authority of our Lord Jesus Christ, to live in harmony with each other. Let there be no divisions in the church. Rather, be of one mind, united in thought and purpose" (1 Corinthians 1:10).

THE GOSPEL IS PERSONAL

When we read that the Holy Spirit told Philip to leave his multitude of new converts and preach to a single individual, we might wonder just what the Holy Spirit was thinking. We find the answer in Jesus' parable of the lost sheep, where the shepherd leaves the ninety-nine in his flock to search for the one that has strayed. Then Jesus says, "There is more joy in heaven over one lost sinner who repents and returns to God than over ninety-nine others who are righteous and haven't strayed away!" (Luke 15:7).

God doesn't see us as mere cogs in a wheel; he sees us as distinct, valuable individuals. In his famous comparison of the church to a body, Paul emphasizes the significance of each individual member. Just as each limb and organ is critically important to the body— whether a hand, an eye, an ear, or a foot—God places the same value on each person in Christ's church (1 Corinthians 12). You are as precious to him as you would be if you were the only person in the world. Had you indeed been the only person in the world, he still would have left heaven to die for you.

The Responses to the Gospel

The conversion of the Ethiopian eunuch demonstrates the three responses to the gospel that lead people into the body of Christ. First, he responded with belief. Scripture says he confessed his newfound belief that Jesus Christ is the Son of God.

Second, after the eunuch confirmed his faith in Christ, he was baptized. As soon as he saw a body of water, he pulled over the chariot and asked Philip to baptize him. In the book of Acts, all the accounts of conversion follow this pattern of immediate baptism. Today, some people choose not to be baptized until long after they declare their belief. But according to the biblical model, once people have come to belief and confessed their faith in Christ, they should follow these New Testament examples and be immersed immediately. This marks the beginning of a new life lived under a new name and a new power.

Third, the eunuch responded with a change of behavior—from a perplexed, unsure seeker to someone who was committed to Christ and full of joy. He was ready to begin living a changed life and do the bidding of the Holy Spirit, who now filled him.

The Success of the Gospel

Just as Paul was considered to be the apostle to the Gentiles, we might call Philip the evangelist to the outcasts. He directed his ministry to people who, for one reason or another, were not accepted or respected by society. And as Acts 8 tells us, his ministry was immensely successful.

One of the keys to Philip's success was his willingness to submit immediately and totally to the guidance of the Holy Spirit. He obeyed, whether the job was big or small, whether he was called to public ministry or private teaching, whether he was sent to a thriving city or a barren desert. It didn't matter to Philip; if the Spirit said, "Go there and do this," that's exactly where he went and what he did. And he did it immediately, without dallying around. Had he hesitated or taken a day off before heading to Gaza, the Ethiopian eunuch would have been long gone when he arrived. The Holy Spirit is a first-rate schedule coordinator, and if we expect to travel with him, then we must board when he calls us.

This sensitivity to the Holy Spirit's leading is key to living by the power of God. It's not always easy to hear his voice since he doesn't usually speak to us in audible ways. We must learn to heed that inner impulse that prods us to do something we hadn't planned for purposes we might not understand. And it's imperative that we obey that impulse immediately. It may be a prodding to meet a need that cannot wait.

C. S. Lewis tells of such an experience:

Some years ago I got up one morning intending to have my hair cut in preparation for a visit to London, and the first letter I opened made it clear I need not go to London. So I decided to put the haircut off too. But then there began the most unaccountable little nagging in my mind, almost like a voice saying, "Get it cut all the same. Go and get it cut." In the end I could stand it no longer. I went. Now my barber at that time was a fellow Christian and a man of many troubles whom my brother and I had sometimes been able to help. The moment I opened his shop door he said, "Oh, I was praying you might come today." And in fact if I had come a day or so later I should have been of no use to him. It awed me; it awes me still.[3]

We must take care, of course, when it comes to heeding impulses. It's all too easy to listen to the wrong nudges or to justify what we want to do based on the fact that we have an inkling to do it. Two keys will help us discern the difference.

1. **Are you living your life in true submission to the Holy Spirit?** Do you pray continually and hold in your heart a strong desire to submit to his will? Over time, have you built up a history of doing what you should do instead of what you want to do? Or, to sum it up, do you have an authentic working relationship with God? If you can honestly answer yes to these questions, it's likely that you will know which impulses are from the Spirit and which ones spring from your own desires.

2. **Do you immerse yourself in the study of the Bible?** Do you have an overall knowledge of God's written Word and how it applies to your life today? If so, this knowledge will be a tremendous help in determining the Spirit's leading. If anything you feel prompted to do conflicts with a biblical principle, you can be sure it's not from God.

As we submit to the leading of the Holy Spirit and God's Word, we can expect God to bless us with more opportunities for ministry. Notice that in Acts 8 the reward for successfully completing a task given by God is often to be given another task. Immediately after Philip's two successful ministries, the Holy Spirit snatched him up and set before him yet another challenge. Philip plunged into his new work with the same drive and enthusiasm, preaching in one town after another and leaving behind him a trail of new churches and joyful believers.

Philip's ministry vividly illustrates the principle of Jesus' parable of the ten servants in Luke 19. The employer in this parable placed a sum of money in the care of each of the ten workers; then he left on a journey. When he returned, he rewarded those who had invested his money and earned a return, saying, "To those who use well what they are given, even more will be given" (Luke 19:26). Jesus was speaking of the reward in heaven waiting for those who are diligent in putting to use the talents God has given them.

May the story of Philip inspire us all to exercise that kind of obedience.

CHAPTER 8

THE MAN WHO
SAW THE LIGHT

✝ ✝ ✝

An Enemy of Christ
Becomes a Friend

Acts 8:1-3; Acts 9:1-19

ONE OF THE PRIMARY FORCES behind the fierce persecution that drove Philip and many other believers from Jerusalem was a young Pharisee named Saul. Saul began taking up the sword against believers when the raging members of the Sanhedrin dragged Stephen out of Jerusalem to be stoned. Saul stood watching the execution, pleased to see one of these Jesus-following heretics get what he deserved. He knew the Jewish law inside and out, and stoning was the prescribed punishment for such a blasphemer. Eager to facilitate the process, Saul invited the council members to toss their robes at his feet, freeing their arms to hurl the stones.

The son of a Pharisee, Saul followed in his father's footsteps, eventually becoming one of the most zealous of all the Pharisees. Though he was born in Tarsus as a Roman citizen, he was a pureblood Jew. He possessed a genius-level mind and had been sent, probably around age thirteen, to study under the great Jewish teacher Gamaliel. He had surpassed all his peers in his knowledge of Jewish law and traditions. Now, at only about thirty years old, Saul was already a leader among the Jews. He likely wasn't a member of the Sanhedrin yet, but he was no doubt aiming for a seat on it one day.

Saul endorsed not only the stoning of Stephen but also any other measures that would destroy these enemies of the Jewish religion. He looked on with satisfaction as Stephen fell under the barrage of stones. He saw Stephen's bloodied face glowing like that of an angel and heard his dying words begging God to forgive his executioners. But that wrenching plea did not penetrate the shell of legalism that encrusted Saul's heart. On the contrary, the scene only whetted his desire to see these enemies of Judaism wiped from the face of the earth.

Acts 8:1 sets the scene for the kind of opposition the early believers faced: "A great wave of persecution began that day, sweeping over the church in Jerusalem." And it was Saul, the eager, young devotee, who was at the forefront of the attack. "Saul was going everywhere to destroy the church. He went from house to house, dragging out both men and women to throw them into prison" (Acts 8:3).

With Jerusalem under control, "Saul was uttering threats with every breath and was eager to kill the Lord's followers" (Acts 9:1). He was determined to pursue those who had fled to other cities and complete the purge with a mop-up operation. He received authorization from the high priest to lead a contingent of men to the Syrian city of Damascus to arrest believers and bring them back to Jerusalem for execution. With a warrant in hand, Saul eagerly set out on the 150-mile journey.

I have to wonder what was going through this fanatic's mind as he traveled. Saul was a conscientious man, so we can be sure he was convinced he was doing the right thing. Yet later in Scripture, we find hints that something deep in his conscience was pushing against this conviction. Though his emotions were hardened against these followers of Jesus, it hardly seems possible that he could shut out the joy he saw on Stephen's face as he died or the words of forgiveness Saul heard him utter in his final moments. Saul didn't allow such thoughts to interfere with his mission, but no doubt they kept prodding quietly, pushing toward the surface of his mind.

Under Divine Arrest

Then something happened that Saul, a man who liked to be in control, never could have predicted. As Saul approached Damascus, a light brighter than the sun suddenly shone all about him. It was like being inside a sustained flash of lightning. The light knocked him to the ground, blinding him to everything but the figure of a man standing within it (1 Corinthians 9:1).

"Saul, Saul, why are you persecuting Me?" the man said.

"Who are You, Lord?" Saul cried.

"I am Jesus, whom you are persecuting. It is hard for you to kick against the goads."

Saul stared in terror, trembling violently. "Lord, what do You want me to do?"

DAMASCUS

Damascus is said to be the oldest continually inhabited city in the world, having a recorded history of four thousand years. It has been the capital of several nations, and today it is the capital of Syria. Damascus is first mentioned in the Bible in connection with Abraham's war with four kings (Genesis 14:15). In ancient times, Damascus was a cosmopolitan city, an intersection for caravans from all directions carrying exotic treasures of spices, perfumes, fabrics, carpets, and wine (Ezekiel 27:18). Like Israel, western Syria, which includes Damascus, was part of the Roman Empire in Saul's day.

"Arise and go into the city, and you will be told what you must do" (Acts 9:4-6, NKJV).

The men with Saul gaped in wonder. They'd heard the voice, but they couldn't see anything. Only Saul had seen the blinding light and the man within it.

He picked himself up from the ground, opened his eyes, and found that he was completely blind. His companions led him by the hand into Damascus and took him to the home of a man named Judas.

For three days, Saul remained in total darkness. His hosts offered him food and drink, but his world had just been turned upside down, and food was the last thing on his mind. I have to imagine that he was thinking, *How is it possible that I have been wrong all my life?* After spending a lifetime immersed in Jewish law and custom, after preparing himself for a career in Jewish law and leadership, it couldn't have been easy for him to think about relinquishing such an investment of time, energy, and emotion. No doubt he did some desperate soul-searching to convince himself that what had just happened was a product of his imagination.

But Saul could not escape the truth: the vision was real. His blindness was proof. He'd had an encounter with the very Jesus he had been warring against. Those suppressed pangs of conscience that had unsettled his mind were the "goads" Jesus had said he was resisting. The truth of Christ had been prodding him like the pointed sticks that wagon drivers thrust at the legs of their oxen, spurring them to pick up the pace.

At last, Saul gave in. He didn't know what lay in his future, but he knew it would be nothing like what he had planned. His career as an inquisitor was over forever. All he could do was place himself in God's hands and follow whatever path he set him on. He had no idea what his next step would be, but he prayed that God would reveal it to him.

WHAT DID SAUL SEE?

Over the years, some people have contrived various scenarios to discredit the miraculous nature of Saul's vision. Some say he fell from his horse and injured his head, bringing about hallucinations. Others claim that the noonday sun reflecting off the white buildings of Damascus blinded him. Other theories point to sunstroke, a nervous breakdown, or an epileptic seizure. Another idea is that Saul's suppressed guilt acted on his brain to create a crisis-producing illusion. But after studying Saul's conversion in great detail, attorney George Lyttleton wrote, "The conversion and the apostleship of St. Paul alone, duly considered, [is] of itself a demonstration sufficient to prove Christianity to be a Divine revelation."[1] The strongest evidence of the miracle Saul experienced is that his life utterly changed after the incident. Nothing but a miracle could account for such a drastic reversal.

Two Corresponding Visions

The answer to Saul's prayer came in the form of another vision. He saw a man named Ananias coming to him, laying his hands on Saul's head, and healing his blindness. The fact that God was sending this man certainly meant he was a follower of Jesus, and Saul may have found that fact somewhat unsettling. Ananias would see him as an enemy. Would he take him as a prisoner and seek retribution? Would the believers do to him as he would have done to them?

Ananias, meanwhile, was going about his usual business. He had no idea what God was about to ask him to do. Ananias was a Jew who had come to faith in Jesus, quite possibly as an indirect result of Saul himself. Some believers no doubt fled to Damascus to escape persecution in Jerusalem and spread the Good News there. Ananias may well have been one of their converts—one of the very people Saul had come to Damascus to destroy.

Even before his conversion, Ananias was a godly man who was dedicated to Jewish law. Though he was now a believer in Jesus, he maintained a good reputation among the Jews in Damascus (Acts 22:12). His relationship with both the Jewish and the Christian communities may explain why God singled him out as his ambassador to Saul. Saul's Jewish host would admit him, and he could give Saul the godly ministry he desperately needed.

As Saul was receiving his vision about Ananias, Ananias received a vision about Saul. The Lord gave Ananias explicit instructions about what he was to do, even down to the name and street address of the man who owned the house where he was to go. Then came the heart

PAUL'S CONVERSION

The story of Paul's conversion is so important in the New Testament that it is recorded five times:

1. Acts 9: Luke records the event as part of the history of the early church.
2. Acts 22: Paul defends himself before the Jews in Jerusalem.
3. Acts 26: Paul recounts his conversion when he appears before the Roman governors Festus and Felix.
4. Philippians 3: Paul recaps his spiritual journey in a letter to the Philippian church.
5. 1 Timothy 1: Paul shares his testimony with Timothy.

The emphasis the New Testament places on this event indicates the monumental impact Paul had on the church. Over and over in his epistles, Paul returns to this moment on the road to Damascus, and it seems as if all his letters reflect the passion that was sparked in him when he was struck blind by the glory of Christ.

of the message: "When you get there, ask for a man from Tarsus named Saul. He is praying to me right now. I have shown him a vision of a man named Ananias coming in and laying hands on him so he can see again" (Acts 9:11-12).

Though Ananias was a dedicated man ready to do God's will, he wasn't sure he had heard the assignment correctly. "But Lord," he exclaimed, "I've heard many people talk about the terrible things this man has done to the believers in Jerusalem! And he is authorized by the leading priests to arrest everyone who calls upon your name" (Acts 9:13-14). Ananias was a bit like Jonah. Would God really want him to go and help his enemies?

The believers in Damascus knew all about Saul. Many had fled his murderous fury in Jerusalem, and news of his pursuit of Christians had reached Damascus. God understood Ananias's concerns and didn't rebuke him for expressing them. He explained his intent: "Saul is my chosen instrument to take my message to the Gentiles and to kings, as well as to the people of Israel. And I will show him how much he must suffer for my name's sake" (Acts 9:15-16).

Ananias trusted his Lord. God said, "Go," so he went. God's assignments are not always safe, but they are always to be obeyed.

The Great Turnaround

Ananias knocked on Judas's door and was ushered in to see the man he dreaded meeting. But when he looked at Saul, he saw nothing of the fire-breather who had been the church's worst enemy. There he sat, perhaps the most forlorn and dejected human being he had ever laid eyes on. Surely at that moment, all of Ananias's fears dissolved into pity.

"Brother Saul," he said, "the Lord Jesus, who appeared to you on the road, has sent me so that you might regain your sight and be filled with the Holy Spirit" (Acts 9:17).

Immediately something like scales fell off Saul's eyes. His sight returned, and he looked into the face of the very man he had seen in his vision.

Then Ananias delivered his message: "The God of our ancestors has chosen you to know his will and to see the Righteous One and hear him speak. For you are to be his witness, telling everyone what you have seen and heard. What are you waiting for? Get up and be baptized. Have your sins washed away by calling on the name of the Lord" (Acts 22:14-16).

Saul didn't hesitate. He got up immediately, and Ananias baptized him. This man who had lived in darkness his entire life now emerged into the light of God. His appetite returned, and he devoured his first meal in three days.

It must have seemed strange for Saul to hear Ananias address him as "Brother Saul." Three short days ago, he had been determined to eradicate men like Ananias from the face of the earth. Now he was a brother in Christ. Saul's former enemies were now his friends, and his former friends were now his enemies. His entire existence had suddenly been turned upside down. He must have wondered what would come next. What new surprises did God have waiting on the horizon?

✛ ✛ ✛

How to Turn a Life Around

Why did God choose Saul? Of all people to pick as his messenger to kings and rulers and Gentiles, why would he select one who was such a ferocious enemy of his church? God could have annihilated such a man and consigned him to the deepest hell. Instead, he called him to be a leader of the people he had wronged.

The Power of Passion

Although Saul had championed the wrong cause, God knew the core of Saul's character. He was a man of strong passion who threw himself completely into what he believed. When he thought that Judaism was the epitome of God's truth, he immersed himself in it, becoming an expert in every facet of the law.

God appreciates passion. Christ told the church in Laodicea, "I know all the things you do, that you are neither hot nor cold. I wish that you were one or the other! But since you are like lukewarm water, neither hot nor cold, I will spit you out of my mouth!" (Revelation 3:15-16). Apathy makes God sick. Whether the cause is right or wrong, passionate people care about what they believe in. Apathetic people do not. When passionate people are redirected to a right cause, nothing will stop them from going all out for what they believe.

Saul became one of the greatest leaders and most influential figures in the history of Christianity. He wrote thirteen of the twenty-seven New Testament books—almost three times as many as the second most prolific writer, John. He conducted at least five missionary tours, traveling through Asia Minor, Greece, Syria, Italy, Spain, and other nations around the Mediterranean. He trained other missionaries, such as Timothy and John Mark, and established countless

THE HOUND OF HEAVEN

Francis Thompson's poem *The Hound of Heaven* compares God's pursuit of us to that of a bloodhound after a hare. We run from him, chasing our own desires. But we soon find that the objects we pursue—wealth, fame, power, and pleasure—do not satisfy. It's only when God captures us in the embrace of his love that we realize he is the one we desired all along. We tend to chase shadows in pursuit of the true but hidden object of our longing—the very one who is pursuing us. Saul thought he was the hunter, when in reality he was the hunted. And when God caught him in his net, Saul found precisely what he'd been hunting for.

churches, many of which he continued to revisit and mentor through his letters.

God told Ananias that Saul would suffer many persecutions for speaking out about Christ. And indeed, he endured more than his share. He spent at least five years of his life in prison. On five separate occasions he was scourged with lashes, and three times he was beaten with rods. He was stoned, run out of town, shipwrecked three times, and bitten by a snake once. Finally he was martyred, executed by Nero in the mid-60s A.D.

It would be easy to conclude that all this was payback for his terrible persecution of the church. But it was not. God knew it would take someone with Saul's zeal to accomplish the tasks set before him and endure all the obstacles along the way. Passion perseveres in spite of opposition. It sacrifices for what it believes.

The Five Steps of Conversion

We can track the conversion of Saul through five distinct stages. These are the same steps each of us takes when we submit to Christ. Examining these stages can help us understand more about ourselves and our relationship to God.

1. CONFRONTATION

There is always a conflict of wills when a person becomes a Christian. Ever since the fall of Adam and Eve, we humans have been determined to run our own lives and do things our own way. Saul (who later went by the name Paul) puts it this way: "The sinful nature is always hostile to God. It never did obey God's laws, and it never will. That's why those who are still under the control of their sinful nature can never please God" (Romans 8:7-8). This explains why we so often resist when confronted with the gospel. We don't want to give up our self-will. What God chooses for us may not be what we would choose for ourselves. God confronts us with an all-or-nothing proposition: we can follow his way or not at all. He accepts no half-hearted commitments.

Saul's confrontation with God was a miraculous encounter because God had a special role for Saul: he was to be one of his apostles, carrying the message of Jesus Christ to nations throughout the Middle East and Europe.

Our confrontations with the Lord are not always so dramatic. They may come in a church service when the pastor quotes Scripture or makes some statement that reaches into our hearts and convicts us of sin. An encounter with God may come from reading the Bible or another book, or through a traumatic experience such as a serious illness, an accident, or a significant loss.

For the former unbeliever C. S. Lewis, a confrontation with God came during a conversation with a hardened atheist friend. As his friend discussed the evidence for the historicity of the Gospels, he privately admitted, "It almost looks as if it had really happened once." Lewis was thunderstruck. If this cynic of cynics was not safe from the reach of God's hand, who was? Lewis had adamantly resisted conversion, not wanting to give up his ingrained habits and pet sins. Though he continued to kick against the goads, he could not escape. He soon fell to his knees and admitted that God was God, calling himself "the most dejected and reluctant convert in all England."[2]

2. CONVICTION

The miracle of the blinding light and the image of Jesus Christ made it impossible for Saul to dismiss the encounter as an illusion or a dream. And the fact Jesus himself was speaking to him immediately put him under conviction. He had been wrong. He was guilty. Those people he had been persecuting were right. The Resurrection was an absolute fact, for Saul had now seen the resurrected Christ. When Jesus asked, "Why have you been persecuting me?" Saul realized that every blow and every cruelty he had inflicted on the church, the body of Christ, was a blow felt by the body's head, Christ himself.

There comes a moment for all of us when we realize we are out of alignment with the standard of right and wrong that permeates all creation. It may hit when we feel guilty over some wrong done to a friend, a loved one, or even a stranger. It may occur when we realize we have a harmful habit we can't break or a temptation we can't resist. Many churches have prison ministries that are highly successful because the inmates are painfully aware of their guilt and their need for forgiveness.

Conviction is always a low point. It comes when people realize what they are—individuals who have defied God, enemies of the Maker of the universe. But conviction is ultimately a good thing, because it shows us our need for change and for God's help. It brings us to the point where there is nowhere to go but up.

3. CONVERSION

Conversion is a complete change from one thing to another. Perhaps you've seen a residence converted into a retail store, a vase converted into a lamp, a garage converted into an office or a den, or a railway car converted into a diner.

Conversion from a self-ruled sinner to a Spirit-filled Christian happens when a person faces a confrontation with God and is moved by the conviction to yield to God's Spirit. It's a metamorphosis from one kind of being to another—a transformation as dramatic as a caterpillar becoming a butterfly. It's a change from an earthbound life ruled by worldly appetites to a soaring life filled with joy and beauty. It's a change from self-absorption to outflowing love. It's a change from "It's all about me" to "It's all about God."

God invites all of us to make this kind of change. What he asks of us is that we will submit to him and allow him to reshape our lives into forms that are fit for eternity.

4. CONSECRATION

"Lord, what do You want me to do?" (Acts 9:6, NKJV). That was the first question Saul asked after the figure in the light identified himself as Jesus. It is exactly the right question for all of us who have confronted Jesus, faced the conviction of our guilt, and chosen to submit to God. With this question, we are essentially saying to God, "Now that I know who you are, I want you to direct me. What would you have me do?"

By asking this question, Saul displayed his willingness to devote himself fully to God and follow wherever he led. That is the meaning of consecration. To consecrate means "to devote or dedicate to some purpose." From his conversion forward, Saul became the quintessential example of a life consecrated to God.

This turnaround was monumental for Saul. He had been his own master, a leader in the Jews' war against Christians. He would have enjoyed success and esteem among the Jews had he stayed on his previous course. But as John MacArthur notes, "God crushed Saul, bringing him to the point of total consecration. From the ashes of Saul's old life would arise the noblest and most useful man of God the church has ever known."[3]

Once we have encountered Christ, the only rational response is to fall down and ask, "Lord, what do you want me to do?" We've joined his cause. He is our commander. Our only option now is to ask for our assignment and consecrate ourselves to his service.

5. COMMUNION

As Saul sat immobile during his three days of blindness, we can only imagine the whirlwind of fears and confusion that must have swirled through his mind. He was isolated as never before. After his encounter with Christ, he could no longer be part of his former circle of friends and colleagues, nor was he a member of the community of Christians. Knowing about his past, they might refuse to accept him. They might even turn the tables and deal harshly with him out of retribution. All at once he was friendless and alone, caught in a no-man's-land between former friends and former foes.

But in those three days of darkness, Saul prayed. He communed with God as never before. And God answered his prayers with exactly what he needed—a new friend and a new community. Ananias welcomed Saul into his life and commended him to the church in Damascus. After some understandable uncertainty on the parts of both Saul and his new family, they embraced him with the overarching love that flowed from Christ. Saul had found his place—a community where he could serve and love and find real joy.

The Power of Transformation

In the late 1800s, a man named Mel Trotter lived a fairly unremarkable life. He was the son of a bartender who drank almost as much as he served. Mel followed his father's footsteps into alcoholism. He became a barber and got married, trying to convince the world he had his life together. He concealed his addiction for years, eventually causing his wife and son deep hurt when the truth came out. Unable to hold a job, Trotter went on binges, abandoning his family for weeks at a time.

One day he came home from a ten-day drinking binge and found his two-year-old son dead in his wife's arms. Guilt and self-loathing almost drove Trotter to suicide. Instead, he sold the shoes off his feet to buy something to drink and made his way to Chicago. He staggered into a Chicago mission, where he was converted to Christianity after hearing the testimony of its director, a reformed alcoholic.

Mel stopped drinking, spent every night at the mission, and in time was called to Grand Rapids, Michigan, to direct a newly founded mission there. The mission was highly successful, and Trotter went on to found a large chain of missions throughout the United States, which still operate successfully today.[4]

You may think your life is too riddled with sin or you have done things so terrible that you are beyond the possibility of transformation. The stories of Saul and the thousands of Mel Trotters who have been changed throughout the history of the church should wipe that thought from your mind. Changed lives like these show that God can work miracles in people who to us seem beyond hope.

Some Christians allow memories from their past to rise up and cause doubt. *Has God really forgiven me for what I did to that person? The fact that I still feel remorse must mean I'm not forgiven. Maybe I'm not saved.* But God's forgiveness is deeper than we can grasp.

John Newton, who wrote "Amazing Grace," the most famous Christian hymn of all time, was someone whose transformation seemed impossible. An unbeliever who embraced an immoral lifestyle as a young man, Newton became a captain of ships that carried slaves packed into the holds under the most miserable conditions. His encounter with God came during a storm at sea. Sinking seemed inevitable until he prayed and the ship was saved.

After his conversion, Newton became an Anglican priest and an abolitionist who influenced the young William Wilberforce to stay

PAUL THE APOSTLE

Saul (soon to be called Paul) was an apostle of Jesus Christ, just like the twelve who were called while Jesus was on earth. According to the qualifications for an apostle, this meant he had to have seen Christ and been appointed by him. Saul met both qualifications during his encounter with Jesus on the Damascus road. As he told the church in Corinth, "Last of all, as though I had been born at the wrong time, I also saw him. For I am the least of all the apostles" (1 Corinthians 15:8-9). That encounter confirmed Saul as an apostle. He had seen Jesus, and Jesus had called him to do his work.

the course in the House of Commons until the slave trade was finally abolished.

In the 2006 film *Amazing Grace*, John Newton is portrayed as a man deeply haunted by the memories of the twenty thousand maltreated slaves carried on his ships. Yet he knew he had been forgiven. The terrible memories remained, but the guilt had been taken away. As he later wrote,

> *Amazing grace! How sweet the sound*
> *That saved a wretch like me.*
> *I once was lost, but now am found,*
> *Was blind, but now I see.*

Yes, memories of our past wrongs will remain with us. It's the way our minds work. And our adversary is an expert at pulling up those dark moments from our pasts and parading them through our heads to convince us that our conversions were not real.

But we must not confuse memory with guilt. Even Saul remembered the evil actions of his past, and he mentions these events several times in his letters. Those memories continued to cause him pain, but they didn't destroy his assurance of salvation. In writing to his young protégé Timothy, Paul expressed his desire that others would see in his life the grace God showers on even the worst sinners who repent and turn to him:

> I used to blaspheme the name of Christ. In my
> insolence, I persecuted his people. But God had mercy
> on me because I did it in ignorance and unbelief. Oh,
> how generous and gracious our Lord was! He filled me
> with the faith and love that come from Christ Jesus. This
> is a trustworthy saying, and everyone should accept it:
> "Christ Jesus came into the world to save sinners"—and

I am the worst of them all. But God had mercy on me so that Christ Jesus could use me as a prime example of his great patience with even the worst sinners. Then others will realize that they, too, can believe in him and receive eternal life.   1 TIMOTHY 1:13-16

The grace of God overcomes all sin. *All* sin. The memories of sin no longer hold us captive; they are merely reminders of what Jesus Christ has swept away.

CHAPTER 9

STORMY BEGINNINGS

✝ ✝ ✝

A Former Enemy
Redirects His Zeal

Acts 9:19-31

IT MUST HAVE BEEN QUITE A SHOCK for the church in Damascus when Ananias introduced them to Saul on the Sunday following his conversion. Did they respond with fear? Wonder? Joy? Resistance? Hospitality? A combination of all these reactions must have rippled through the assembly. Could such a vicious enemy really have been converted? Or was he merely pretending in order to flush them out?

Whatever the initial reaction, the Damascus church soon accepted Saul as one of their own. He needed their fellowship. He needed their forgiveness and affirmation. He needed to know that when he turned his back on his former life, he was not suspended in a no-man's-land where he was neither friend nor enemy, Jew nor Christian.

Once accepted, Saul was not the type of person to sit quietly in the pew while his heart was bursting with the news he had to tell. His allegiance had changed, but his zeal had not. The Jews—his lifelong friends and the people who shared his heritage—needed to hear that what they had been resisting was really true: Jesus was the resurrected Messiah. Saul had experienced this truth firsthand, and he couldn't let them remain in the darkness of their ignorance. He knew he was just the one to tell them. After all, he was one of them—a respected leader who was well educated and thoroughly grounded in Jewish laws and traditions. Surely they would listen to him.

Immediately Saul began to visit the Jewish synagogues in Damascus. His work in decimating the believers in Jerusalem was known everywhere, and no doubt these Jews were honored to have such a famous leader address them. Apparently news of his conversion to Christ had not yet gotten around, or the doors would have been bolted against him.

When Saul began to preach, the Jews were stunned. They expected him to rail against the upstart Christians who were stealing converts from the Jews in every city. Instead, he told them about Jesus, saying, "He is indeed the Son of God" (Acts 9:20).

Saul, a novice Christian at this point, couldn't have known much about the inner workings of Christianity yet. But the simple message of Christ's resurrection had power of its own, without being dressed up in the trappings of theology. At this point he did by necessity what he did deliberately much later, when he was addressing the church in Corinth: he preached the message of Christ in its simplicity. As he told the Corinthians, "I didn't use lofty words and impressive wisdom to tell you God's secret plan. For I decided that while I was with you I would forget everything except Jesus Christ, the one who was crucified" (1 Corinthians 2:1-2).

The Jews were just as baffled as the believers in Damascus were when he showed up at their doorstep. The Jews murmured to one another, "Isn't this the same man who caused such devastation among Jesus' followers in Jerusalem? And didn't he come here to arrest them and take them in chains to the leading priests?" (Acts 9:21).

The confusion and uncertainty stirred up by his preaching may have led Saul to realize that he wasn't ready to preach yet. He decided to leave Damascus for the time being. As he explained in one of his letters, "I did not rush out to consult with any human being. Nor did I go up to Jerusalem to consult with those who were apostles before I was. Instead, I went away into Arabia" (Galatians 1:16-17).

Why Arabia? We aren't told, but the context of Saul's statement gives us a possible hint. He says that he didn't go to Jerusalem to consult, which indicates he felt a need for advice—for more knowledge and more wisdom in proclaiming his faith. He chose not to go back to Jerusalem to learn under the apostles, because his life would be in danger there. His former colleagues would see him as the worst of traitors. And his presence among the believers remaining in Jerusalem would endanger them as well. Rather than risking his life and the lives of the believers in Jerusalem, he went into the desert to consult with God.

Although we don't know where in Arabia Saul went, in his letter to the Galatian church he mentions Mount Sinai, the holy mountain of God, as being in Arabia (Galatians 4:24-25). The Sinai Peninsula is not technically in Arabia, but at this time the two locations would have been closely associated. God had spoken to Moses on Sinai, and the prophet Elijah had escaped to Sinai, where God spoke to him in a time of crisis and discouragement. Quite possibly, Saul followed the example of these biblical figures and spent a portion of his three years of isolation in Arabia near God's holy mountain.

It's safe to assume that during this time of study and prayer, Saul would have become astute in the theology of his new religion, connecting the dots between Old Testament prophecies and their fulfillment in Christ. After three years in Arabia, Saul returned to Damascus and once more began to preach in the Jewish synagogues.

The Jewish leaders grew alarmed as members of their synagogues began to drift into the Christian camp. Clashes erupted between those who converted and those who resisted. The Jewish leaders couldn't defeat Saul by persuasion or argument, so they did as the leaders of the Sanhedrin had done when facing the apostles in Jerusalem: they resorted to sheer power.

The governor of Damascus joined the Jews who were determined to put an end to the turmoil by killing Saul. The governor ordered the garrison of soldiers in Damascus to arrest him on sight. Shifts of guards were posted around the clock at the city gates, making it impossible for Saul to escape without falling into their hands (Acts 9:23-24).

Some of the believers in Damascus, however, got wind of the plot and informed Saul. Obviously they no longer doubted the sincerity of his conversion. If his former colleagues were out to murder him, the change in him had to be real. So they devised their own counter-plot. In the dead of night, they furnished Saul with travel provisions, secured a rope and a large basket, and eased him down from a high window in the city wall. This time Saul traveled directly to Jerusalem.

MOUNT SINAI

Mount Sinai is a rugged peak jutting some 7,500 feet above sea level. It's located at the lower end of the semi-barren Sinai Peninsula, between Egypt and Arabia. Its name in Arabic is *Gabal Mūsā*, meaning "Mount of Moses." This is the site of the burning bush God used to speak to Moses, the place where the Israelites camped after escaping the wrath of Pharaoh, and the mountain where Moses received from God the stone tablets containing the Ten Commandments. The newly freed Israelites feared this mountain. Scripture tells us that its smoke-shrouded peak rumbled with thunder, flashed with fire, and quaked violently (Exodus 19:16-20). When Moses descended the peak after forty days in the presence of God, his face literally glowed. Mount Sinai was a significant location in Israel's history, for Jews and Christians alike.

The Believers in Jerusalem Reject Saul

Upon arriving in Jerusalem, Saul immediately found where the believers were meeting and introduced himself as one of them. They didn't believe him for a minute, and it's easy to see why. Unlike the believers in Damascus, who accepted him after only a brief hesitation, the believers in Jerusalem had suffered directly from Saul's ruthlessness. He had decimated the church after Stephen's death, throwing many of the believers into prison, where they were subsequently condemned to death. Those who escaped his net had fled the city, as Philip did, and scattered in all directions.

They simply didn't believe that a man who had caused so much devastation could change—especially to the point of joining the side he had formerly tried to annihilate. Surely his conversion was a ruse. They thought he was trying to infiltrate the church, gleaning as much inside information as he could—the places where the believers met and the whereabouts of Christians in other cities. So they shut their doors on Saul.

The poor man needed an advocate—someone the believers trusted who could vouch for the genuineness of his conversion. Thankfully, when there is a need, God provides. He sent just the right man to open the doors of the church in Jerusalem to Saul. Barnabas the encourager, whom we discussed in chapter 5, saw the good side of everything, including people. He was also an exemplary believer who was completely dedicated to Christ and the community of believers in Jerusalem.

When Barnabas caught wind of Saul's rejection, he found Saul and listened to his story. Barnabas saw that Saul's conversion was real, and he took him directly to meet the apostles. Had it not been for Barnabas, Saul might never have been accepted into the company of believers in Jerusalem.

Barnabas introduced Saul to Peter and James, a brother of Jesus who had become a prominent leader of the church in Jerusalem. If his stint in Arabia was Saul's education, his time in Jerusalem was his internship. Peter took Saul under his wing for a couple of weeks while they traveled around preaching, setting an example for Saul about how to articulate the Good News. No doubt Peter took Saul along for another reason as well: to give Saul his stamp of approval. His endorsement would certainly open doors that were previously shut to him.

Another Plot against Saul's Life

While traveling with Peter, Saul didn't ease up in his zeal for the message of Christ's resurrection. Throughout the tour, he preached "boldly in the name of the Lord" (Acts 9:28). Once again, his boldness incited opposition that got him into trouble. At one stop, he held a debate with some Greek-speaking Jews, and his insistence that the resurrected Jesus was the Messiah offended them deeply. Like the Jews in Damascus, they plotted to kill him.

Saul knew nothing about the plot until he was praying in the Temple and saw a vision of Jesus standing before him. He had appeared to Saul to warn him of the threat against his life.

SEA TRAVEL IN THE FIRST CENTURY

Thanks to Rome, sailing the Mediterranean was safe from pirates, but it wasn't convenient. First, passengers packed tents, food, and supplies for the entire voyage. Next, they traveled to the port of departure and stayed at an inn while searching for a ship bound for their destination. They had to haggle over the fare with the captain, load their supplies, and wait for departure, which could take days, depending on weather and omens. All ships were merchant vessels, and only the wealthy had cabins. Everyone else camped on deck, braving weather and sea spray. There was no food service, but passengers could prepare their own food in the ship's galley. The day of arrival was always uncertain, subject to wind and weather.

"Hurry! Leave Jerusalem," he said, "for the people here won't accept your testimony about me" (Acts 22:18).

The danger meant little to Saul. He told Jesus he wanted to stay and tough it out.

But the Lord insisted: "Go, for I will send you far away to the Gentiles!" (Acts 22:21)

Jesus had an altogether different plan for Saul. While Saul was prepared to remain in Jerusalem preaching to his fellow Jews, God was preparing him for the work he is known for today: taking the gospel of Christ to non-Jews throughout the Mediterranean world.

When the believers in Jerusalem learned about the plot against Saul's life, they hustled him out of the city and escorted him to the seaport town of Caesarea. There they put him on a ship sailing for Tarsus, Saul's hometown at the northeast corner of the Mediterranean Sea.

Saul arrived safely in Tarsus and remained there for the next seven years or so. This period of Saul's life is often referred to as the "silent years," because nothing is recorded of his activities during this time. He doesn't appear again in the book of Acts until chapter 13, where he is referred to as Paul, the Greek equivalent of the Hebrew name Saul. The name change is appropriate, for it signals the nature of the ministry Saul would engage in for the rest of his life. He would become known as the apostle to the Gentiles.

✝ ✝ ✝

AFTERSHOCKS OF CONVERSION

What Saul experienced on the Damascus road was a spiritual earthquake. It was a visual, audible, emotional, and supernatural intervention in his life. Nothing was the same for him after that monumental encounter. The aftershocks of his conversion shook the world during his lifetime—and continue to do so today.

Not everyone experiences such a radical conversion as Saul's. Most of us don't see bright lights and hear the audible voice of the Lord. So what can we learn from Acts 9? There are at least three lessons we can learn from the reverberations of Paul's conversion that will help us today, no matter where we are in our spiritual journeys.

The Value of Patience

A cursory reading of Acts 9 might lead us to assume that Paul (let's go ahead and use the name he's commonly known by) began a successful ministry immediately—one that flowed seamlessly from his conversion into missionary tours, church planting, and instructive letters to churches and his protégés. But when we consider the autobiographical details he reveals in some of his letters, we can see that his ministry didn't unfold that way. In his early years of serving Christ, Paul experienced three periods of seclusion, each longer than the one before. He spent three days blind and isolated in Damascus, three years somewhere in Arabia, and about seven years in his home city of Tarsus.

Given Paul's intense nature, God knew he needed these periods away from the world to get his feet firmly planted before he shot out of the starting block and raced into his ministry. God had to slow Paul down long enough for him to absorb the necessary knowledge and wisdom to become the great apostle he was destined to be.

When a task is set before us that fits our skills and kindles our enthusiasm, we often feel a strong impulse to jump in with both feet and depend on our instincts and excitement to carry us through. But plunging in without preparation isn't usually the wisest or most efficient way to complete a task. If you've ever bought an item that required assembly, such as a child's swing set or a piece of furniture, it's tempting to pull out the screwdriver and wrench and dive in, ignoring the tedious step-by-step instructions. But you're likely to start at the wrong end first or miss a step that was a necessary prerequisite to a part you've already assembled. Then you have to back up, disassemble the part you spent half an hour on, and go back to the beginning. Although reading the instructions requires some investment, it saves time and frustration in the long run.

The enthusiasm of new Christians is something wonderful to behold. Many converts want to jump right into ministry, often begging church leaders for a great task to tackle. But that enthusiasm may need to be temporarily diverted. Not stifled, but redirected into learning, study, and training. This doesn't mean they should lose their enthusiasm or let it evaporate into apathy. Instead, that zeal should be channeled into preparation for a time.

Christian leader and author J. Oswald Sanders explains why this is so important: "'God is anxious that His children get a good education,' wrote Dr. S. D. Gordon. Every man He has used has had a course in the university of Arabia, a wilderness training. Joseph, Moses, Elijah, John the Herald, Paul . . . even the divine Son Himself in the days of His humanity—these are a few of the distinguished graduates. . . . The marked results are broad perspective, steady nerves, keen eyesight and insight. There come utter dependence on

SAUL'S SILENT YEARS

We are not told what Saul did in those seven years when the church sent him to his hometown of Tarsus to escape the murderous Jews in Jerusalem. In 2 Corinthians 6 and 11, he offers a grim litany of the hardships he endured: imprisonments, exhaustion, mob violence, sleeplessness, hunger, beatings with rods and with lashes, stonings, cold weather with inadequate clothing, and three shipwrecks. Knowing Saul's zeal and tenacity, he no doubt spoke in the synagogues in Tarsus, where he would have encountered many acquaintances from his past. It could well be that some of his beatings and floggings occurred as a result of his preaching there.

God, utter independence of man, childlike simplicity, warm sympathy and deep humility. But the highest degree goes to patience, the rarest trait of all, most God-like, hardest and longest to acquire."[1]

If you need precedents for patience in preparation, consider Moses, who spent forty years herding sheep in the backcountry of Midian before God called him to his great work of leading the Israelites out of slavery. Jesus himself spent forty days in the desert between his baptism and the beginning of his ministry.

Let these examples, along with Paul's three periods of isolation, encourage you to exercise patience and let God do his deep work in your life as he prepares you to be a useful tool in his hand.

The Need for Community

Isolation in order to pray and commune directly with God has real value. We read of Jesus making an effort to spend time alone for that very purpose. Paul's three days of secluded prayer before he got his sight back readied him for the message and ministry Ananias brought to him. If Paul did indeed go to Mount Sinai after escaping Damascus, there's no doubt God made contact with him there.

But this principle of seclusion, valid and valuable though it is, carries with it a caution and a limitation. We often hear people say things like, "I don't need to go to church to be a good Christian. I find God when I'm fishing on the lake or hiking in the mountains or gazing at the rolling waves on a seashore." God is in all these places, of course. He is everywhere. But private, individual communion with him was never meant to be the totality of our religious experience—and certainly not a way of life.

When Elijah discovered that Israel's wicked queen Jezebel was intent on killing him, this discouraged and burned-out prophet escaped into the wilderness and then to Mount Sinai. God spoke to him on the mountain, renewed his strength and courage, and assured him that he was not alone in his struggle against idol worship in Israel. God told him that he had reserved seven thousand godly people who had never bowed to the Canaanite idol Baal. Then he sent the renewed and encouraged Elijah to civilization again—back into the fellowship of believers—to take up his ministry with renewed energy and vision (1 Kings 19:1-18).

The same was true for Jesus. After he got away from the crowds to pray, he always came back and resumed his ministry. And we can be sure that when Paul went to Arabia, he didn't spend the entirety of those years on Mount Sinai. That would have been a temporary retreat, after which he went back into the populated areas of the country to find God's people. We know there were Christ followers in Arabia, because Arabs had been among those converted at Pentecost (Acts 2:11).

Christianity cannot be lived in isolation; it is a religion of fellowship. In chapter 7, we saw that Paul, in one of his letters, compared the church to a body. Specifically, he called it the body of Christ. Christians are united as one, connected to one another by the sinews and ligaments of fellowship and sustained by the lifeblood of Jesus that flows through each person.

As the apostle John wrote, we cannot claim to love God if we do not love our fellow believers. "If we don't love people we can see, how can we love God, whom we cannot see?" (1 John 4:20). And we can't love our fellow believers if we don't demonstrate that love through our actions. We must be with them in order to be a part of them. A primary function of church is to nurture, support, assist, comfort, and love our fellow believers as if we were all parts of the same body—which, in fact, we are.

True, it's refreshing to get away from the busyness of our world and retreat to the mountains, the lake, or the seashore. But those getaways are not where we live. We are called not to isolation but to community, and after a period of refreshing, we return to our homes and resume our responsibilities. The same is true of our involvement in the church. We need to take time-outs and isolate ourselves for prayer and communion with God to refresh our souls and recharge our spirits. But this retreating is not the essence of our relationship with God. The Christian life is not a getaway; it's the place we come back to, the place where we live with our lives plugged in to one another. To isolate ourselves from fellowship with other Christians is like severing a branch from a vine. It will wither and die without the vine's sustaining nutrients flowing through it.

It's clear that after his conversion, Paul desired fellowship with other believers. Ananias immediately introduced him to the believers in Damascus and smoothed the path to his acceptance. After returning to Jerusalem, he met with the fellowship of believers there and eventually won their confidence through Barnabas's intervention.

The rejection Paul experienced must have been painful. But he was committed to being a working part of the living body of Christ, so he kept knocking at that closed door. He refused to be deterred by church members who didn't live up to their own standards of love and acceptance.

The Power of Encouragement

Barnabas's name appears more than thirty times in the book of Acts, so it's obvious that he was instrumental in the growth of the early church. As we study his life, it's easy to understand why he made such an impact. He was a born encourager.

Encouragement is defined as "the act of inspiring others with renewed courage, renewed spirit, or renewed hope." Encouragers take the courage they have and let it flow through them to someone who desperately needs it. That's precisely the kind of person Barnabas was.

We may be able to define encouragement with words, but we come to truly know it when we experience it through someone's life and example. In the book of Acts, Luke gives us a window into the ministry of Barnabas, showing us that the life of an encourager is marked by generosity and graciousness.

ENCOURAGERS ARE GENEROUS

When we first encounter Barnabas, he is giving money for the benefit of others. Barnabas sold a piece of his property and then gave the proceeds to the apostles for the church in Jerusalem. He opened his hands and released what was his for the benefit of others—the hallmark of a generous person.

Wherever generosity abounds, encouragement also abounds. Barnabas built others up not only with his words but also by helping to meet their needs.

ENCOURAGERS ARE GRACIOUS

Barnabas was the first believer to extend grace to the apostle Paul when he was introduced to the church in Jerusalem. After Paul's conversion, when he went to Jerusalem to meet with the other apostles, they were initially afraid of him.

But there was one person who reached out to Paul and welcomed him into the church: Barnabas. His acceptance of Paul communicated this important message: "I forgive all that's in the past. Just as God has extended grace to you, so do I."

Barnabas was also there to encourage John Mark years later when he hit rock bottom after deserting Paul and Barnabas on a missionary journey. When the two senior apostles were going out for a second journey, Paul refused to take John Mark along since he had deserted them on the first trip. But Barnabas extended grace to the young man and invited him to journey to Cyprus with him, continuing their missionary work and John Mark's apprenticeship in the faith. Barnabas saw potential in John Mark that just needed to be developed. He put his arm around the young man's shoulders and encouraged him not to give up (Acts 15:36-41).

Barnabas's ability to encourage others didn't come from his own merits, however. The Holy Spirit is the ultimate encourager. He is the one who counsels and encourages us from within, so it's only logical that a person who is filled with the Holy Spirit would be an encouraging person.

This story from almost one hundred years ago paints a beautiful picture of the power of encouragement:

In 1921 Lewis Lawes became the warden at Sing Sing prison. No prison was tougher than Sing Sing during that time. But when Warden Lawes retired some 20 years later, that prison had become a humanitarian institution. Those who studied the system said credit for the change belonged to Lawes. But when he was asked about the transformation, here's what he said: "I owe it all to my wonderful wife, Catherine, who is buried outside the prison walls."

Catherine Lawes was a young mother with three small children when her husband became the warden. Everyone warned her from the beginning that she should never set foot inside the prison walls, but that didn't stop Catherine! When the first prison basketball game was held, she went . . . walking into the gym with her three beautiful kids and she sat in the stands with the inmates.

Her attitude was: "My husband and I are going to take care of these men and I believe they will take care of me! I don't have to worry." She insisted on getting acquainted with them and their records. She discovered one convicted murderer was blind so she paid him a visit. Holding his hand in hers she said, "Do you read Braille?"

"What's Braille?" he asked. Then she taught him how to read. Years later he would weep in love for her.

Later, Catherine found a deaf-mute in prison. She went

to school to learn how to use sign language. Many said that Catherine Lawes was the body of Jesus that came alive again in Sing Sing from 1921 to 1937.

Then, she was killed in a car accident. The next morning Lewis Lawes didn't come to work, so the acting warden took his place. It seemed almost instantly that the prison knew something was wrong.

The following day, her body was resting in a casket in her home, three-quarters of a mile from the prison. As the acting warden took his early morning walk he was shocked to see a large crowd of the toughest, hardest-looking criminals gathered like a herd of animals at the main gate. He came closer and noted tears of grief and sadness. He knew how much they loved Catherine.

He turned and faced the men, "All right, men, you can go. Just be sure and check in tonight!"

Then he opened the gate and a parade of criminals walked, without a guard, the three-quarters of a mile to stand in line to pay their final respects to Catherine Lawes. And every one of them checked back in. Every one![2]

That is the power of an encourager. I don't know of anything we need more today than encouragers—a whole host of Barnabases to build one another up. The world can be a discouraging place, but God didn't intend for us to struggle through this life alone. He has given us one another so that his courage and his hope might flow from us to the world.

CHAPTER 10

THE LIFE GOD BLESSES

✛ ✛ ✛

Peter's Personal Ministry Tour

Acts 9:31-43

WHILE THE FIERCE PERSECUTOR SAUL had been terrorizing the believers in Jerusalem, the church was in a continual state of turmoil. Believers fled the city and scattered throughout Judea, Galilee, Samaria, Syria, and other distant lands. But when Saul himself became a believer, "the church then had peace throughout Judea, Galilee, and Samaria" (Acts 9:31).

Though the decimation of the church was traumatic and disruptive, it had positive long-term effects. For one thing, it spurred the good news of Jesus Christ to take root in other cities and provinces. In addition, the peace that followed the persecution seemed to trigger a new burst of energy in Jerusalem. The persecuted believers had plumbed the depths of their commitment, and when the trouble ended, that commitment expressed itself in a burst of evangelism powered by the Holy Spirit. The church became even stronger and grew in numbers.

Another Miraculous Healing

With the crisis over, the apostles no longer had to remain in hiding and spend their time and energy on chaos control. Peter decided it was a good time to leave Jerusalem and head out on a tour of pastoral care. He traveled to several of the towns where the believers in Jerusalem would have relocated, no doubt to see how they were faring and to encourage them in their faith.

When these believers left Jerusalem, the umbilical cord had been severed. They no longer had a daily connection to the apostles and leaders of the established church in Jerusalem. We can be sure that Peter wanted these believers to know that they were still one church—all part of the larger body of Christ and all connected by their common bond of love for one another and for God.

At one of Peter's stops, he came to the town of Lydda and met with the believers there. This must have been a happy reunion with many people he had known in Jerusalem. While in the city, he was introduced to a man named Aeneas. We aren't told much about Aeneas other than his name and his condition. Eight years earlier, Aeneas had become paralyzed either by disease or by accident, and he could not walk. He was totally bedridden.

We don't know if this man was a believer. Perhaps he was the friend or neighbor of a Christian who led Peter to the man's bedside, hoping for a healing miracle. Or Peter may have preached while in Lydda, and this man could have been in the crowd, carried there on his cot.

Whoever Aeneas was and however he and Peter met, this meeting had significant repercussions that rippled throughout the town. When Peter saw the paralyzed man lying helpless on his mat, he said, "Aeneas, Jesus Christ heals you! Get up, and roll up your sleeping mat!" (Acts 9:34).

Aeneas was healed instantly. It was much like Peter and John's healing of the lame man by the Temple gate. Though Aeneas had been paralyzed for nearly a decade, his atrophied legs now surged with instant power and muscle tone. He was able to walk immediately, without having to relearn balance and muscle control. Aeneas stood, rolled up his mat, and walked away as if he had never been injured.

The people of Lydda had never seen anything like it. Here was a man who had been bedridden for eight years and who was now completely healthy. It was clear that an astounding miracle had occurred, and the man who had performed the feat attributed it entirely to the power of Jesus Christ.

There's no doubt that these people had already heard of Jesus, as news of his crucifixion and rumors of his resurrection had spread far beyond Jerusalem. The disciples who had fled from Saul's persecution surely would have recounted the story as well. Now the people were witnessing confirmation of what these newcomers had been proclaiming. It must be true: Jesus Christ had risen from the dead. The healing of Aeneas proved that Jesus was alive and very much involved in the affairs of people.

The citizens of Lydda reacted quite differently from the Jews in Jerusalem when Peter had healed the lame man at the Temple gate. Here, no one arrested him. No one dragged him off to the council for trial and imprisonment. In fact, their reaction was just the opposite: the entire population of Lydda and those living in the surrounding area in the Sharon Plain turned to the Lord and became believers. This private act of healing produced enormous and far-reaching results.

A Woman of Grace . . . and a Tragic Death

In the nearby port town of Joppa lived a Jewish woman named Tabitha, who had become a believer in Christ. Tabitha was her Aramaic name, but the Greek translation was Dorcas—the name she is typically known by today. Both names mean "gazelle," which in the poetry of the Middle East was an animal often associated with feminine grace and beauty.

THE TOWN OF LYDDA

Lydda was located in Judea, about ten miles inland from the Mediterranean coastal town of Joppa. After the Israelites conquered Canaan, the tribe of Benjamin founded the town and named it Lod. At the crossroads of trade routes from Jerusalem to Joppa and Babylon to Egypt, Lod became a hub for caravans stopping to replenish supplies and repair equipment. The repair and manufacturing skills that developed to serve these caravans gave the area its nickname: "the valley of craftsmen." Exiles returning from Babylon rebuilt Lod in the fifth century B.C. It was subsequently conquered by the Greeks and then the Romans, along with the rest of Israel. Today Lydda, adjacent to Tel Aviv and home to the Ben Gurion Airport, is still a transportation hub.

Dorcas lived up to her name. Her benevolent deeds radiated the beauty of her generous and caring spirit. She was a gifted and prolific seamstress who made coats, robes, head coverings, and all other types of clothing for the widows in the church of Joppa. It's likely that she was a woman of some means, which enabled her to invest time and materials into her ministry. Some scholars have speculated that she was a widow herself and that her husband had left her with a substantial amount of money.

Dorcas's skills were humble and didn't reap widespread adulation or public accolades. After all, people don't tend to think of seamstresses as having far-reaching influence. But that didn't matter to Dorcas. It was something she was able to do, so she did it—quietly, efficiently, and consistently, without expecting reward or applause. This unassuming, charitable woman with a spirit as beautiful as a gazelle was an invaluable asset to the widowed believers in Joppa.

One day Dorcas became ill. And instead of getting better, she became progressively worse until she died. The distressed women of the community washed her body for burial, but rather than proceeding to the next step—wrapping the body with embalming spices—they laid it in an upstairs room. This move was highly unusual, as it was customary to wrap a dead body immediately. Without the sophisticated embalming techniques available today, bodies could not be left in the open for any significant length of time.

The reason for this departure from custom was that some of the believers knew Peter was in the nearby town of Lydda. News of the healing of the paralytic had spread, and the believers also would have known that Jesus had raised a widow's son from the dead. Was it possible that Peter might be able to raise Dorcas? It was worth holding off on the preparation process until he could be contacted.

The church sent two men to Lydda to find Peter. They pleaded with him to drop everything and accompany them to Joppa, and he agreed. They took Peter to the home of Dorcas, whose body awaited him in the upstairs room.

Peter could hear the wailing of the widows as he climbed the stairs. Though the common custom of the day was to hire mourners, that wouldn't have been necessary for Dorcas. The mourning of the women gathered around her body was real and unscripted. Peter entered a room filled with the grieving widows. Upon seeing him, they gathered around to show him the coats, robes, headpieces, and other items of clothing Dorcas had made for them.

Peter looked at Dorcas's body lying on the bed and asked the mourning widows to leave the room. He may have wanted it quiet so he could focus on his prayers of supplication. Or maybe he didn't want to draw their attention to his own activity, which might lead them to give the glory for this miracle to him instead of to God. Or perhaps he was remembering when Jesus had cleared the room of people before he raised Jairus's daughter from the dead.

He may have simply wanted to follow the pattern set by his master (Mark 5:40).

When the room was cleared, Peter knelt down and prayed. After some time in communion with God, he stood, turned to the body on the bed, and said, "Get up, Tabitha" (Acts 9:40).

She opened her eyes, and when she saw Peter standing beside her, she sat up, alive again and fully healed from the disease that had caused her death. He reached out his hand and helped her stand beside the bed. Then he called in the widows and other believers who had been waiting outside. They came into the room gaping in amazement but filled with unspeakable joy at seeing their beloved Dorcas alive again and glowing with health.

News of the event spread quickly, and many who heard it or saw Dorcas alive became believers themselves. A dead woman could only have been brought back to life by the power of Jesus Christ, who had defeated death by his own resurrection. Again, Peter's

THE TOWN OF JOPPA

Joppa is an ancient Israeli city located on the Mediterranean coast. We don't know exactly how old it is, but the Egyptian Pharaoh Thutmose lists Joppa among his conquests in the fifteenth century B.C. When the Israelites conquered and divided Canaan in about 1228 B.C., the tribe of Dan inherited Joppa (Joshua 19:40-48). King Hiram floated cedar logs from Lebanon to Joppa for the construction of Solomon's Temple (2 Chronicles 2:16). Ezra used the port for the same purpose when the Israelites reconstructed the Temple after returning from exile in Babylon (Ezra 3:7). The prophet Jonah sailed from Joppa for Tarshish before ending up in Nineveh (Jonah 1:3). Joppa, now called Jaffa or Yafo, is presently part of Tel Aviv. It lost its status as a primary seaport to the ports of Ashdod and Haifa.

private ministry generated ripples that spread to accomplish even greater things.

Peter didn't leave Joppa for a while. He stayed in the home of a believer named Simon, who was a tanner of hides. Tanning was considered an unclean profession to the Jews, who were forbidden to touch the bodies of dead animals. But as we will see in the next chapter, Peter's acceptance of Simon served as a prelude to something greater to come.

✝ ✝ ✝

WHAT KIND OF PERSON DOES GOD USE?

When God has a task to be performed, you might think he would assign it to an idle person who has time to do it. But it seems to be the opposite. He likes to use people who want to work. People who are proactive and are motivated to get things done. People who don't sit around and wait for things to happen but instead make things happen.

CLOTHING IN BIBLE TIMES

Almost all clothing worn in ancient times was made of wool or flaxen linen. Weaving cloth on looms was a professional trade, but women did the actual making of clothes in the home. In poorer families, women would be involved in the entire process, from the spinning of the fibers into thread to making fabric on small looms to coloring fabrics with dyes made from plants or soft stones they crushed themselves. Women also cut out fabric pieces and sewed them together. The clothing people wore was very simple, consisting of loincloth undergarments, tunics, light or heavy cloaks, robes of various weights, shawls, and headwear—either plain for work or decorative for special occasions.

Peter was one of those people. He was always on the move, and sometimes his energy would burst forth in the form of impulsive actions and statements. Once, when he was tired of sitting around waiting, he told the other disciples, "I'm going fishing." Later, when he saw Jesus standing on the Galilean shore, he jumped out of the boat and swam to him (John 21). Awed by the transfigured presence of Moses, Elijah, and Jesus, Peter blurted out that he wanted to build monuments to each of them (Matthew 17:1-4). When Jesus was arrested in Gethsemane, Peter lashed out with his sword, determined that Jesus would not go down without a fight (John 18:10).

Early in his life, Peter's energy was random and immature, but God channeled it for good. After the Holy Spirit filled Peter on Pentecost, that energy was harnessed for a productive ministry that was highly instrumental in the early church.

After things settled down following the persecution of the church in Jerusalem, Peter refused to sit around and take a breather. He launched out into Judea and Samaria, checking on the believers in the churches there. In making this move, Peter demonstrated several important attributes of people who are used by God.

God Uses Humble People

Ever since Pentecost, Peter was the acknowledged leader of the church, the go-to man for Christians in Jerusalem and beyond. Not only was he the leader of the other apostles, but he was also an effective preacher whose sermons had already drawn thousands of people into the faith. He was a highly visible figure in the early church, admired by the believers and a prime target of the church's enemies.

But then this important leader and speaker, who wielded influence over thousands, struck out on his own to visit fledgling churches in rural towns. He didn't go with an entourage or bodyguards. He didn't invite reporters to swarm around him and publicize his successes. He didn't line up dignitaries and supporters to welcome him upon his arrival.

Peter's sole purpose was to see if he could be of any help to the Christians displaced by persecution in Jerusalem. His actions communicated a deep level of humility. Peter didn't have an elevated sense of his own importance; he saw himself merely as a servant of Christ. Whether the job was large and sweeping or small and confined, he was delighted to do it.

Peter's humility was displayed in his willingness to minister in private situations. In this chapter, we see him focusing on individuals, both in the healing of Aeneas and in the raising of Dorcas from the dead. Scripture doesn't record him preaching in either Lydda or Joppa (though he may well have done so). If he did, those sermons were apparently not the most important events of his ministry in these cities. The highlights were his humble, one-on-one contacts with ordinary individuals.

Peter's humility was further demonstrated by his care in deflecting the glory away from himself and onto Christ. Peter was not the healer; he was merely an instrument in the true healer's hands. He went to great lengths to make sure that was clear to his observers.

No matter what call we've been given—whether we're caring for widows or preaching sermons or sewing clothes—God wants us to serve with humility, giving him the glory and acknowledging that anything we have to offer is ultimately a gift from him.

God Uses Available People

Twice in Acts 9, Peter is moved to leave one ministry and take up another. First, he left his position of leadership in Jerusalem to set out on his tour to various churches. We can be sure it was the Holy Spirit who moved Peter to do this. Second, Peter was called to leave

Lydda and travel to Joppa. Although it was people who delivered the call, these men were merely agents of the Holy Spirit. On both occasions, Peter didn't hesitate. He pulled up his stakes and moved on to the next task God had for him.

As Christians, we must learn to be "rootless"—in the best sense. That is, when God sets out a task for us, we must not become so comfortable or attached to what we're doing that we close ourselves off to a different task or a different place in the future.

Often the reward for work well done is to be given yet another task. In C. S. Lewis's book *The Horse and His Boy*, Shasta, the boy, has just completed a long and grueling trip across a vast desert to warn a good king of an impending attack. His companion is wounded, and their two horses are spent when they arrive at the home of the Hermit of the Southern March at the edge of the desert. Shasta wants to collapse and recover from his ordeal, but the Hermit tells him he cannot. He must go on immediately. "If you run now, without a moment's rest, you will still be in time to warn King Lune."

The story continues,

> Shasta's heart fainted at these words for he felt he had no
> strength left. And he writhed inside at what seemed the
> cruelty and unfairness of the demand. He had not yet learned
> that if you do one good deed your reward usually is to be set
> to do another and harder and better one. But all he said out
> loud was:
> "Where is the King?"[1]

Shasta was an example of the apostle Paul's admonition to the Galatians: "Let's not get tired of doing what is good. At just the right time we will reap a harvest of blessing if we don't give up" (Galatians 6:9). We may think we've already done all that should be required of us. But the Christian life is one of self-sacrifice. When another call comes, we must go, knowing that God will bless us for being available to him.

God Uses Dependent People

Peter knew he didn't have the power to raise Dorcas from the dead. It could only be done by the power of God. He sent the widows out of the room and prayed fervently for God to return this woman to life. It was an expression of his complete dependency on God and his power.

It would have been easy for Peter to allow his recent successes to go to his head, leading him to think he had this Christian thing all figured out. I've seen it happen to many Christians, including pastors. The more we think we accomplish "for God," the more we forget that it's really God who is accomplishing his will through us.

Every sincere prayer is an expression of dependence on God. If we fail to pray, we are by default expressing the opposite. We're essentially saying, "I don't need you to run my life; I can do it very well myself, thank you very much." We often fail to realize how outlandish such an attempt at independence really is. Prayer is the Christian's Declaration of Dependence, and we must not grow lax in the practice of it.

Sometime in the late 1800s, five young people went to London's Metropolitan Tabernacle to hear the great Charles Spurgeon speak. They arrived early and found the doors locked, so they sat on the steps and waited. Soon a man strolled up and asked what they were doing. They explained, and in reply he asked if they would like to see the heating apparatus of the church. With nothing better to do, they agreed. The man led them downstairs, beneath the building. At the end of a long hallway, they entered a room filled with seven hundred people, all praying. "This," Charles Spurgeon said to his surprised guests, "is the heating apparatus of this church."

Spurgeon was making a statement of his dependency on God. He knew his church was touching the world not because of him or his preaching but because of what God was doing.

God Uses Flexible People

In the final verse of Acts 9, we read, "Peter stayed a long time in Joppa, living with Simon, a tanner of hides" (Acts 9:43). This little verse has greater significance than one might think. A tanner dealt with the bodies of dead animals—skinning them, scraping their hides, and treating them with solutions that transformed them into pliable leather. Tanners were considered unclean by Jewish law because of their continual contact with dead animal bodies (Leviticus 11). They were denied access to synagogues and were considered outcasts by Jewish society.

Yet Peter, born and raised under Jewish law, was willing not only to associate with this tanner but also to be his guest for an extended period of time. While many Jews had trouble flexing on any point of the law, Peter had learned from his master's association with the outcasts of his day (such as Samaritans, tax collectors, prostitutes, and lepers) that people were more important than legalism and traditions.

Peter would have remembered what Jesus had told the Pharisees who complained that Jesus was violating the Jewish law by healing on the Sabbath: "The Sabbath was made to meet the needs of people, and not people to meet the requirements of the Sabbath" (Mark 2:27). Now Peter was applying that principle on a broader level and accepting people who were considered outcasts by the law's rigid interpreters. Peter was flexible enough not to get stuck in the misguided traditions of the past.

His flexibility was soon to be tested to the extreme, as we will see in the next chapter. His association with Simon may have been a preparatory step to get him ready for that test.

When God calls us to do something outside our comfort zones, are we open enough to say yes? Or do we cling so tightly to the way we've always done things that we miss the joy of serving and connecting with others who are different from us?

A Ministry of Kindness

The work Dorcas did was neither spectacular nor public, like much of Peter's ministry was. But in one way, it was quite similar. Peter had temporarily left his highly visible ministry for one-on-one service to ordinary people in ordinary places. Dorcas's ministry was also a quiet one, serving ordinary people. While the power of God might not be as obvious in her needle and thread as it was in Peter's leadership and preaching, it was certainly there. When it comes to ministry and service to others, God is in the small things as fully as he is in the big things.

All of us have known Dorcases in our time—ordinary, behind-the-scenes servants of God who use their talents in small ways without receiving glory or applause. In God's estimation, these quiet, humble servants are great saints in the church. While their ministry may seem small from a human perspective, it is far from ordinary to God.

I recently heard about a ninety-nine-year-old woman who had suffered two strokes and could barely get around, even with the help of a walker. For years, her hands had been painfully arthritic, with knuckles and joints swollen into knotty lumps and fingers that couldn't flex without pain. This woman had devoted her life to sewing and mending clothing for others. The effects of her strokes and arthritis made this work impossible, so she took up knitting. The best she could do with her damaged hands was to make dishrags. So, she made dishrags. Working day after day over the years, she made hundreds of dishrags, all brightly colored and durable. She gave them away to anyone who came to visit and sent others to friends and relatives.

Now, dishrags may not be highly valuable commodities, but everyone with a home needs them. This dear woman didn't worry that her ministry seemed small and insignificant. She continued to make dishrags because, in her diminished condition, that was the one thing she could do. It was her ministry, and I can assure you that God was in it.

The Far-Reaching Effects of Small Deeds

Chaos theory is a mathematical principle that says the behavior of dynamic systems is highly sensitive to initial conditions. An illustration of this principle is the butterfly effect, which suggests that the volume of air displaced by the wings of a butterfly can, weeks later, influence the formation and trajectory of a tornado.

Like falling dominoes, every action causes a chain of reactions that ripple through time and influence the future in unpredictable ways. Many people have seen a marvelous example of this principle in the classic movie *It's a Wonderful Life,* starring James Stewart and Donna Reed. Unexpected events force George Bailey to abandon his dream of becoming an architect and spend his life in his little hometown, Bedford Falls, running the family's struggling building and loan business.

A crisis occurs when earnings from the business are lost. The bank will go under, and George, though innocent, will be charged with a felony. Thinking his life has been a complete failure, he decides to kill himself so his insurance policy will provide for his family. But an inept angel named Clarence prevents the suicide and shows George how different things would be had he never been born. Without George to save him from drowning, his brother wouldn't have been able to prevent the deaths of everyone on a transport ship during the war. Without George to stop him from making a fatal mistake, the community's druggist would have spent twenty years in prison and sunk into hopeless alcoholism. Without George as her husband, Mary Hatch would have trudged through life as a lonely, single woman. Without George to keep the building and loan business open, the evil Mr. Potter would have taken over Bedford Falls, turning it into a shantytown of squalid homes and corruption.

George Bailey had thought his life was a failure. He never became the architect of those great buildings of his dreams. But as the angel showed him, every little good thing he did created a ripple effect over time, resulting in enormous blessings.

When the apostle Peter healed a man in a seemingly insignificant town, he didn't know that this one deed would cause the entire city and the valley around it to come to the Lord. When he prayed for the return of Dorcas's life, he didn't know that raising this one woman from the dead would cause so many people in her town to believe that Jesus had risen from the dead.

As Dorcas pulled her needle through the fabric, one stitch at a time, day in and day out, she didn't know that her little acts of kindness would influence believers so much that her death would leave an unfillable void in the church. The arthritic woman knitting dishrags didn't realize how her bright threads and generosity may touch the heart of some discouraged recipient.

Every small act, every deed of kindness—however insignificant it may seem—is of crucial importance. The long-term results can be mind-boggling. That's why each of us must be diligent to do the tasks placed before us with all our hearts, souls, and minds. We must not wait for the big jobs. The small ones are just as crucial. If they don't get done, neither will the big ones. Those small tasks lay the foundation for God to build on.

The old song titled "Little Is Much When God Is in It" eloquently expresses this concept of serving in humble, ordinary ways.

Little is much when God is in it!
Labor not for wealth or fame.
There's a crown—and you can win it,
If you go in Jesus' name.[2]

CHAPTER 11

A WALL COMES DOWN

✝ ✝ ✝

The Conversion of the First Gentile

Acts 10

IN THE FIRST CENTURY, the city of Caesarea was a large, cosmopolitan center for trade, shipping, and Roman and Greek cultures. Most of its citizens followed pagan rituals, including sensual worship at the temples honoring Greek and Roman gods and goddesses. Caesarea was the seat of the Roman governor of Judea and the site of a major Roman military garrison, which served as the base for the Roman legions stationed in Judea.

One of the prominent army officers in the Caesarean garrison was a centurion named Cornelius, who was captain of the Italian regiment. His high position in the Roman military indicates that he must have been tough-minded, disciplined, well trained, and brave. Yet Cornelius was a unique man. Though he lived in a city dominated by paganism and worked in a profession not noted for sensitivity, he was a devout and moral monotheist. He was drawn to the religion of the Jews, as were all the members of his household. The more he learned, the more devout he became. The Bible describes him this way: "He gave generously to the poor and prayed regularly to God" (Acts 10:2).

Though he was a Gentile and an officer of the army that had conquered Israel, the Caesarean Jews came to respect Cornelius for his piety and generosity. He also maintained a disciplined prayer life. This may mean that he attended the Jewish synagogue regularly, though as a Gentile he would have been seated in a separate section and wouldn't have been able to fully participate in the ceremonies.

One afternoon at about three o'clock, Cornelius was deep in prayer when, out of nowhere, a man appeared before him wearing dazzling robes.

"Cornelius," the angel said.

Brave though he was, Cornelius was filled with terror at the unearthly sight. When he found his voice, he asked, "What is it, sir?"

"Your prayers and gifts to the poor have been received by God as an offering! Now send some men to Joppa, and summon a man named Simon Peter. He is staying with Simon, a tanner who lives near the seashore" (Acts 10:3-6).

Cornelius didn't hesitate. The moment the angel left, he called in his military attendant, who was a trusted soldier, and two household servants. He related the entire incident to them and sent them to Joppa with instructions to find Peter and urge him to return with them.

Peter's Shocking Vision

Simon the tanner, Peter's host, lived near the Mediterranean Sea, possibly to keep the odor of his business from offending the citizens of Joppa. The Scripture account indicates that Peter had freedom to treat Simon's house as his own home. Meals were prepared for him, he had access to the flat roof, and he even had permission to entertain his own guests.

It was noon on the day after Cornelius had sent his three messengers on a thirty-mile journey to find Peter, and they were now nearing Joppa. Meanwhile, Peter was hungry, and as the noonday meal was being prepared, he decided to go up to the rooftop to pray. In the midst of his prayer, he fell into a trance. The sky opened above him, and he saw a large sheet being let down by its four corners. All sorts of animals, reptiles, and birds crawled around in the sheet—some of which were considered clean and edible to Jews and others that definitely were not.

Then a voice boomed from heaven saying, "Get up, Peter; kill and eat them."

"No, Lord," Peter said. "I have never eaten anything that our Jewish laws have declared impure and unclean."

But the voice reprimanded him: "Do not call something unclean if God has made it clean" (Acts 10:9-15).

ROMAN CENTURIONS

Centurions were captains of army units consisting of one hundred infantry soldiers. They commanded men both in battle and when they were stationed in occupying zones. Centurions received twenty times the salary of infantry soldiers. Most were promoted from the ranks, and thus were the bravest and best warriors of the Roman army. The New Testament mentions five centurions, all in a positive light: the centurion Christ commended for his great faith (Matthew 8:5-13); the centurion at Jesus' crucifixion who confessed his belief in Jesus (Mark 15:39); Claudius Lysias, who saved Paul from the Jews who were planning to kill him (Acts 23:12-35); Julius, who saved Paul from being executed to prevent his escape from a grounded ship (Acts 27); and finally Cornelius, the first Gentile convert.

After three repetitions of the vision, the sheet was pulled up and the heavens closed on it.

What in the world could that have meant? the perplexed Peter wondered. As he ruminated over the mysterious vision, the messengers from Caesarea arrived at the gate and asked for him.

At that moment, the Holy Spirit said to Peter, "Three men have come looking for you. Get up, go downstairs, and go with them without hesitation. Don't worry, for I have sent them" (Acts 10:19-20).

So Peter went down to meet them and ask why they had come. When they explained their mission, Peter realized that they were Gentiles. For devout Jews, it was unthinkable to have any meaningful association with Gentiles. Yet there they were, begging Peter to accompany them on a daylong journey and to visit the home of a Gentile—and worse, a Roman officer. Yet the Holy Spirit had explicitly told him to go with these men. What could this mean? So far, Peter had preached only to Jews and half-Jewish Samaritans, which was a stretch in itself. Surely God didn't mean for him to preach to Roman Gentiles.

Then a realization hit him, and the meaning of the rooftop vision became clear. Just as the animals God created were no longer to be considered unclean, neither were the Gentiles. God loved them just as he loved the Jews. He wanted the wall that separated them to come down, just as the distinction between clean and unclean animals had been erased in his vision.

Then, no doubt with his heart pounding over this venture into uncharted territory, Peter did something he had never thought he would do. He invited these Gentiles to stay overnight so they could get an early start for Caesarea in the morning.

It's hard for us to comprehend what an enormous leap this was for a man whose entire life had been steeped in Jewish laws and traditions. According to Jews, there were only two classes of people: Jews and everyone else. They considered themselves to be God's chosen people, and with good reason. Their own Scriptures told them so: "You are a holy people, who belong to the LORD your God. Of all the people on earth, the LORD your God has chosen you to be his own special treasure" (Deuteronomy 7:6). It never occurred to them that Gentiles, too, would be invited into a relationship with God. The prophet Jonah went far out of his way to avoid preaching to pagan Nineveh and was troubled when the people turned to the Lord. What the Jews had overlooked was the reason they had been specially chosen by God in the first place: to make the entire world as special as they were by bringing the message of salvation to all people.

Peter should have known this, for he was present when Jesus told the apostles to "go and make disciples of all the nations" (Matthew 28:19). But conditioning and lifelong prejudice sometimes prevent us from comprehending what God is plainly telling us. Peter understood it now, however, so he gathered six men to go with him—all believers from Joppa. He wanted witnesses present to

CLEAN AND UNCLEAN FOODS

Jewish dietary laws designated which foods were acceptable largely based on what was healthiest for a society without modern cooking, sanitary conditions, and medical techniques (Leviticus 11:1-47; Deuteronomy 14:3-21). Edible (clean) mammals had to have cloven hooves and be ruminants—animals that chewed cud. This meant that pigs were excluded; they had cloven hooves but did not chew cud. When it came to birds, Jews could eat birds other than hawks or scavengers. They could eat fish that had both fins and scales (which excluded catfish and eels). They could eat winged insects that could crawl and jump, such as grasshoppers, locusts, katydids, and crickets. One major reason Jews considered Gentiles unclean was because they ate almost anything, making no distinction between clean and unclean foods.

verify what he knew his fellow Jews would find hard to accept. At first light, the ten-man entourage left Joppa and headed down the Mediterranean coast to Caesarea.

An Ancient Wall Crumbles

Cornelius waited eagerly for Peter. He had gathered a small crowd of relatives and friends to welcome Peter and hear what he had to say. I imagine him pacing the floor, checking his sundial every fifteen minutes, and sending servants to look down the road to see if his guest was on his way.

Finally Peter and his entourage arrived. They were ushered inside, and immediately Cornelius fell to his knees to worship his guest. It makes sense that Cornelius would have an elevated sense of Peter's importance. Why wouldn't he kneel to a man who was an envoy of the Lord and had angels arranging his schedule?

But Peter would have none of it. "Stand up!" he said. "I'm a human being just like you!" (Acts 10:26). Peter must have been struck by the incongruity of this whole encounter. Here was a Gentile army commander kneeling before a Jewish fisherman!

When Peter and Cornelius went inside with the other guests, Peter led with a frank statement about the Jewish attitude toward Gentiles. "You know it is against our laws for a Jewish man to enter a Gentile home like this or to associate with you. But God has shown me that I should no longer think of anyone as impure or unclean. So I came without objection as soon as I was sent for. Now tell me why you sent for me" (Acts 10:28-29).

Cornelius replied by recounting how an angel had appeared to him, commending him for his generosity and telling him his prayers would be answered when he sent for Peter. "Now we are all here," he concluded, "waiting before God to hear the message the Lord has given you" (Acts 10:33).

Always ready to preach, Peter needed no further encouragement.

First, he admitted that he had learned something from this encounter. "I see very clearly that God shows no favoritism. In every nation he accepts those who fear him and do what is right" (Acts 10:34-35). Then he told the group the complete story of redemption, beginning with John's ministry. He described Jesus' work throughout Judea and Galilee, combating the oppression of Satan with healings and other miracles. He told Cornelius and his guests about Jesus' crucifixion and resurrection, verifying these events with accounts from many witnesses, including himself.

Peter knew that with Cornelius's connection to the Jews in Caesarea, he was probably aware of the hundreds of prophecies that predicted the coming of the Messiah. He identified Jesus as the one these prophets had spoken of and concluded by saying, "Everyone who believes in him will have their sins forgiven through his name" (Acts 10:43).

Peter's audience got the message; they believed everything he told them. As he was speaking, the Holy Spirit came down and entered the hearts of these Gentiles, and they began speaking in other languages and praising God.

The six Jewish believers who had accompanied Peter could hardly believe their eyes. Was it possible that God's Holy Spirit was being poured out on Gentiles?

Any lingering questions Peter might have had about the entire episode were now put to rest. Gentiles were to be welcomed into the church along with Jews. It was, in essence, a second Pentecost—the Gentile Pentecost announcing the acceptance of the rest of the world into the Kingdom of God.

Peter understood all this, but he knew that his six companions were not as prepared for the revelation as he was. He had received a heavenly command to come to Caesarea for this very purpose. But his friends were still reeling from what they had just witnessed.

Peter asked them, "Can anyone object to their being baptized, now that they have received the Holy Spirit just as we did?" (Acts 10:47).

The answer was obvious, of course, but he wanted his companions to affirm it. They proceeded to baptize Cornelius and his household. The elated Cornelius, desiring to know more about this new faith, invited Peter to stay with him for several more days.

On that day, in the home of a Roman centurion, a virtually impenetrable wall that had separated Jews and Gentiles for more than two thousand years crumbled entirely. As we will see in the next chapter, however, there would still be resistance on the part of many Jews to cross the gap where that wall had stood.

✢ ✢ ✢

SALVATION WITHOUT BOUNDARIES

As a Roman centurion, Cornelius must have been a tough, disciplined, respected leader. These characteristics are vital to officers of any effective army, which certainly included the world-conquering Romans.

Given his position and status, it's amazing that Cornelius was willing to accept the arrogance and disdain with which the Jews treated Gentiles. The gulf between the two groups was seemingly insurmountable. Jews went out of their way to avoid relationships with Gentiles, and when some kind of interaction was necessary, Jews took care not to make physical contact with them.

Jews would never enter the home of Gentiles or invite Gentiles into theirs. Jews couldn't eat food prepared by Gentiles, and if a Jew purchased a cooking or eating utensil from a Gentile, it would have to be purified before use. If Jews walked through a Gentile country, the dust that collected on their sandals was considered defiled, and they would shake it from their feet the moment they returned to their own land. On top of these cultural differences, there was also a significant spiritual gap. Jews considered themselves to be God's chosen people and considered everyone else to be second-class humans—defiled, unclean, and inferior.

The Payoff of Persistence

So why would a highly positioned Roman officer like Cornelius go along with such debasing treatment? Because he was a true seeker. Something in his heart told him that there must be a supreme being, a true God. He must have sensed it in the beauty and order of nature, the magnificence of the heavens, and the wonder of life and love. He was wise enough to discern that there had to be something more than the amoral gods and goddesses of the Roman pantheon.

Somewhere along the way, Cornelius was exposed to the Jewish concept of one God, the creator and sustainer of all that exists. Perhaps this was the God he was seeking. He learned more about the Jewish religion, and what he found attracted him—perhaps not least of all the prophetic promises of a Redeemer who would take away the guilt over sin that every human bears.

We might reasonably presume that Cornelius's first contact with a Jewish leader did not go well. A Gentile Roman army officer would hardly have been welcome in a synagogue. Yet Jews loved to make converts almost as much as they despised Gentiles (Matthew 23:15). So perhaps a rabbi held Cornelius at arm's length while condescending to teach him the rudiments of Jewish theology. The Caesarean Jews may have allowed Cornelius to attend their synagogue meetings, but only as a non-participant, segregated from the Jewish worshipers.

Yet Cornelius persisted. His desire to know God burned hotter than the humiliation of his treatment. As he learned more, he began to pray regularly and help the Jews, providing alms for the poor and support for the synagogue. As a result, the Jews began to respect him as a good and upright man. But he was still a Gentile, and his acceptance would have been partial at best.

Scripture makes it clear that honest seekers find what they are looking for. Cornelius may well have been aware of God's promise to hear the prayers of those who search for him: "If you look for me wholeheartedly, you will find me" (Jeremiah 29:13). Cornelius became a living demonstration of the truth of that passage.

Cornelius was also like the man in the parable of the great treasure. In this parable, Jesus compares the Kingdom of Heaven to a priceless treasure that a man finds while plowing a field. Once he uncovered it, he "sold everything he owned to get enough money to buy the field" (Matthew 13:44). Nothing is of higher value than spending eternity with God in heaven. This reward is worth whatever it costs in terms of money, time, humiliation, pain, or ostracism. Cornelius knew this and had the wisdom and desire to act on it.

Agents of God

God heard the prayers of Cornelius and delivered a message to Peter. Peter is not the only person in Scripture to have a divine encounter like this. But did you ever wonder why the message of salvation

THE CITY OF CAESAREA

Caesarea, originally called Strato's Tower, was built by the Sidonians in the fourth century B.C. It was subsequently controlled by the Greeks and briefly ruled by Israel until Pompey conquered the Jews in 63 B.C. In 30 B.C., Caesar Augustus gave the town to Herod the Great, who commissioned an extravagant construction program that included elaborate palaces, public buildings, a temple to Augustus, an amphitheater, a hippodrome that seated 20,000 people, a theater, and a spectacularly engineered harbor. He renamed the town Caesarea after Caesar Augustus. It was the seat of the Roman government of Palestine, the residence of the governor, and the site of a major military garrison.

wasn't just revealed directly to Cornelius? There's no doubt that after such an imposing, supernatural encounter, Cornelius would have believed. So why did God go through the more complex process of sending two messages to two men, having one fetch the other from a distant city to do what could have been done simply and directly? Let's look at two reasons.

1. GOD USED THIS AS A TURNING POINT FOR THE CHURCH.

God sent Peter to Cornelius for Peter's sake and for the sake of the church as a whole. Peter needed to see this watershed event with his own eyes so he would know without a doubt that God had extended the offer of salvation to those outside the narrowly drawn Jewish circle.

This was important because the church looked to Peter as their primary leader. Jesus himself had told Peter, "I will give you the keys of the Kingdom of Heaven. Whatever you forbid on earth will be forbidden in heaven, and whatever you permit on earth will be permitted in heaven" (Matthew 16:19). When Peter reported the conversion of a Gentile, the church listened.

2. GOD CREATED HUMANS TO BE HIS AGENTS.

God sends us to accomplish his will because he made us for that purpose—to be his agents, his representatives, his regents on earth. After creating the world with all its plant and animal life, God said, "Let us make human beings in our image, to be like us. They will reign over the fish in the sea, the birds in the sky, the livestock, all the wild animals on the earth, and the small animals that scurry along the ground" (Genesis 1:26). He entrusted us with ruling, caring for, and building up this world under the guidance of the Holy Spirit.

Whenever possible, God chooses to accomplish his purposes on earth through men and women rather than through direct intervention. Even when Adam and Eve rebelled and lost their power to represent God perfectly, he didn't withdraw from humans the calling he had created us for.

God could have brought the Israelites out of Egypt without telling Moses to confront Pharaoh and initiate the ten plagues. God could have warned Israel directly about the consequences of their idolatry instead of sending prophets such as Isaiah and Jeremiah. God could have written the Bible himself instead of going through the laborious process of guiding human beings to write it. As C. S. Lewis said, "[God] seems to do nothing of Himself which He can possibly delegate to His creatures. He commands us to do slowly and blunderingly what He could do perfectly and in the twinkling of an eye."[1]

Today we still have the task and privilege of being God's agents. Even though we experience many lapses and much bumbling as we accomplish his will, he is pleased when we serve him with willing hearts. He is like a parent who is delighted with a toddler's first wobbly steps. Though the child doesn't walk perfectly, the parent delights in each attempt and each improvement.

However, the fact that we have fallen natures and can't do God's will perfectly doesn't let us off the hook. As G. K. Chesterton said, "Anything worth doing is worth doing poorly." Imperfect as we are, we are still God's agents. It is our duty and privilege to do his will, even if our attempts are messy and disordered. It's a way to show him our allegiance, devotion, and trust.

The God Who Reveals Himself

I sometimes hear the objection that Christianity is unfair for those who die never having heard of Christ. Christians say that Jesus is the only way to God, which must mean that those who haven't heard the gospel are hopelessly lost through no fault of their own.

The case of Cornelius helps us to answer that objection. We don't know for sure, but it's likely that his first sense of the reality of

God began with nature. The psalmist David wrote that all creation declares his existence:

> The heavens proclaim the glory of God.
>   The skies display his craftsmanship.
> Day after day they continue to speak;
>   night after night they make him known.
> They speak without a sound or word;
>   their voice is never heard.
> Yet their message has gone throughout the earth,
>   and their words to all the world.
>
> PSALM 19:1-4

The apostle Paul says that many people do not find God in the evidence of creation because they "suppress the truth by their wickedness. They know the truth about God because he has made it obvious to them. For ever since the world was created, people have seen the earth and sky. Through everything God made, they can clearly see

THE KEYS TO THE KINGDOM

Jesus told Peter, "I will give you the keys of the Kingdom of Heaven" (Matthew 16:19). I believe these keys refer to the three crucial doors Jesus identified before ascending into heaven. He told his disciples to preach the gospel first to the Jews, then to the Samaritans, and then to everyone else (Acts 1:8). Peter opened all three of these doors. He preached his first sermon to the Jews at Pentecost (Acts 2), he imparted the Holy Spirit to the Samaritans (Acts 8:17), and he opened the door of the Kingdom to the rest of the world when he brought the message of salvation to Cornelius (Acts 10). Just as Jesus had promised, he was using Peter to build his church (Matthew 16:18).

his invisible qualities—his eternal power and divine nature. So they have no excuse for not knowing God" (Romans 1:18-20).

Cornelius didn't suppress this truth, because he was actively searching for God. He was willing to kindle the natural glimmer of light that revealed the existence of a supreme being. He didn't smother it with sensual pleasures or materialistic desires. And because he allowed that light to illuminate his heart, God sent more light to show Cornelius his next step. This led him into contact with the Caesarean Jews, who pointed him to the God he knew must exist. Then he followed that new beam of light as far as it would lead him. His prayers and generosity were signs of his desire to serve and honor God with the light he had been given. Those good works did not save him, but they reflected the state of his heart. Cornelius was ready for more light, so God beamed it on him in the form of Peter, who brought him the pure light of Christ. And in Christ he found the way, the truth, and the life.

God Moved the Wall

The most famous verse in the Bible says, "This is how God loved the world: He gave his one and only Son, so that everyone who believes in him will not perish but have eternal life" (John 3:16). Although God sent Jesus Christ through the Jews and gave them the first opportunity to respond to the gospel, his intention all along was for the offer of salvation to include the entire world.

At first the Jewish believers, including the apostles, did not fully realize how far reaching God's plan of salvation was. Even Peter was reluctant to invite Gentiles into the Kingdom of God. But the Holy Spirit got his attention, and his heart changed. The Jews had walled off the Gentiles, excluding them from God's favor, but Acts 10 shows how God destroyed that wall forever.

During a fierce battle in World War I, a young Protestant chaplain with the American troops befriended a local Catholic priest when they were stationed in Italy. When it was time for his unit to relocate, the chaplain joined them but was killed shortly thereafter. The priest got word of his death and wrote a letter to the army leaders.

"May I have permission to bury the chaplain's body in the cemetery behind my church?" he wrote.

The officials, knowing about the chaplain's friendship with the priest, agreed.

But the priest hit resistance from the church authorities.

"Was he Catholic?" they asked.

"No," the priest replied. "He was Protestant."

"We're sorry," they said, "but you can't bury a Protestant here. This cemetery is for Catholics only."

Many years later, a war veteran from the chaplain's unit visited Italy and found the old priest. After catching up briefly, the American asked to pay his respects at the chaplain's grave. To his surprise, the priest took him to a grave inside the cemetery's fence.

"This is where the chaplain is buried?" the former soldier asked. "You must have gotten permission to move the body!"

The priest shook his head. "They told me where I couldn't bury the body," he said with a smile. "Nobody ever told me I couldn't move the fence."[2]

That's exactly what God did for the Gentiles: he moved the wall to include them. And I'm so thankful that he did, because I am a Gentile. Now all of us can be on the inside of God's Kingdom, regardless of our nationality or heritage.

Are Good Deeds Enough?

In this chapter we were introduced to a deeply moral and religious person. Cornelius gave, prayed, and was respected by the religious people of his day. But as good as Cornelius was, that was not enough. He was still a sinner. His soul carried the infection of the sinful nature we have all inherited. And because of his sin, he bore guilt before God that he could not get rid of on his own. He needed the blood of Christ to atone for his sins, and he needed the resurrection of Christ to give him new life. If his good works had been enough, there would have been no need for God to send Peter to deliver the gospel. Jesus Christ was the only way for Cornelius—and he's the only way for us.

I fear that many good and religious people today are depending on their good works to save them. They do the right things, say the right words, and give to the church and to others, and they think these actions will earn them a place in heaven. This is tragic because it is only by coming to Christ in repentance and claiming his atoning blood that we can be saved. As Peter told the Sanhedrin, "There is salvation in no one else! God has given no other name under heaven by which we must be saved" (Acts 4:12).

If you are doing everything you can think of to live a good and religious life but have not placed your faith in Christ, then you are as lost as Cornelius was. I urge you to do as Cornelius did and seek the Lord. Call a pastor or another strong Christian and let that person do for you what Peter did for the centurion: open the door for you to enter the Kingdom of God.

CHAPTER 12

INTO ALL THE WORLD

✝ ✝ ✝

The Explosion of the Church

Acts 11

THE APOSTLE PETER DREADED THE TRIP TO JERUSALEM, but he could not put it off forever. He knew he would be met with resistance by his fellow Jewish Christians for making the gospel available to the Gentiles. He had stayed in Caesarea at the home of the Roman centurion Cornelius for several days, answering questions about the faith, telling the new Gentile believer about his experiences with Jesus, and passing along knowledge Cornelius would need as he led the new church that had begun in his home. It had been a fruitful time, but Peter knew it was time to head back to Jerusalem.

Peter was determined not to go alone. He would need support—and he would need witnesses to corroborate what had occurred in Caesarea. So he took with him the six men who had accompanied him from Joppa. After bidding warm farewells to Cornelius and his household, the seven men set out on their fifty-mile journey to Jerusalem.

When they arrived, Peter called the church leaders together. The moment he walked into the meeting, he realized that news of what had happened in Caesarea had already reached them. Their glares and stony faces told the whole story: they were not happy. Peter had invited Gentiles into the church founded by the Jewish Messiah, and now he had some explaining to do.

The accusation was quick and direct. To Peter's surprise, it addressed not the overarching theological issue but his own behavior. The first words out of their mouths were, "You entered the home of Gentiles and even ate with them!" (Acts 11:3).

Peter may well have thought, *You believers sound just like the Pharisees who accused Jesus of eating with sinners. If I'm getting the same kind of criticism he got, I must be doing something right.* Seeing his fellow believers so eager to pounce, he chose not to set off a debate. He figured his best approach would be simply to tell them what had happened in Joppa and Caesarea.

He described his own vision of the unclean animals, the arrival of Cornelius's envoys, and the Holy Spirit's command to accompany them to Caesarea. He told about arriving at the home of Cornelius and preaching to Cornelius's family and friends.

Then Peter said, "As I began to speak, the Holy Spirit fell on them, just as he fell on us at the beginning. . . . And since God gave these Gentiles the same gift he gave us when we believed in the Lord Jesus Christ, who was I to stand in God's way?" (Acts 11:15, 17).

Peter's six witnesses confirmed his story, and the leaders of the church in Jerusalem could not refute it. To their credit, they didn't even try. Faced with such clear evidence of God's hand at work, all their objections evaporated. They said, "We can see that God has also given the Gentiles the privilege of repenting of their sins and receiving eternal life" (Acts 11:18). Then they began to praise God for taking the church across this new frontier. Peter must have breathed a sigh of relief.

The Church Establishes an Outpost

Meanwhile, the believers who had scattered from Jerusalem during Saul's persecution traveled to various Mediterranean lands and cities, including Cyprus, Phoenicia, and Antioch of Syria. These refugees carried with them the good news of Christ. But word of Peter's conversion of a Roman had not yet reached them, so they didn't know that the door had been opened to Gentiles. Therefore, they preached to Jews only.

But this constriction soon broke loose. Among the places where the refugee Christians preached was the seafaring province of Phoenicia. Phoenician merchants had active trade routes around the entire rim of the Mediterranean Sea as well as its islands. It's likely that converted Phoenicians carried the gospel to Cyrene on the northern coast of Africa, as well as to other port cities. Some of the believers from Cyrene and Cyprus went to Antioch and, on their own initiative, began preaching to Gentiles. The Holy Spirit was with them in this bold move, and as a result, massive numbers of Greeks became believers.

The believers in Antioch now formed a large church—perhaps the first one that was composed of both Jews and Gentiles. When news of this congregation reached the leaders in the mother church of Jerusalem, they grew concerned. Jews and Gentiles coming together under one roof to worship could create a volatile mix. Would the Jews in Antioch accept these outsiders? Did the believers need further instruction to facilitate the integration? There was only one way to find out. They would send a trusted envoy to Antioch to help with the transition.

The man they chose was one we've met before: Joseph, the disciple from Cyprus whom the apostles nicknamed Barnabas, which means "son of encouragement." This dedicated follower of Christ was deemed just the right person to manage the potentially explosive mix in the church in Antioch.

ANTIOCH OF SYRIA

The city of Antioch was founded by Seleucus, a general under Alexander the Great who eventually ruled the Greek Empire. He named the city after his son and successor, Antiochus I. Legend says that Seleucus gave a piece of meat to an eagle, the bird of Zeus, and built the city on the site where the sacred bird landed to eat the offering. With a population of 500,000, Antioch was the third-largest city in the Roman Empire, and it soon became the capital of Syria. Though many Jews lived in the city, the majority of its citizens were Greeks. In his lifetime, Seleucus founded sixteen different cities called Antioch throughout the empire. One of these, Antioch in Pisidia, is also mentioned in Acts 13.

When Barnabas arrived, what he saw energized him. This church was thriving, actively spreading the Word and bringing in new members as fast as they could be absorbed. Barnabas immediately began to live up to his name. "He was filled with joy, and he encouraged the believers to stay true to the Lord" (Acts 11:23). The church in Antioch couldn't help but love Barnabas. They welcomed him in, seeing that he was a "good man, full of the Holy Spirit and strong in faith" (Acts 11:24).

New converts always need help and encouragement, and this church was no exception. After the euphoria of the initial conversion wanes, people often feel the tug of their former lives and the old temptations they left behind. They may also find that their new lives are harder than they expected, or they may encounter opposition from friends and family. Other new believers may find that the church they thought was an ideal society has its share of problems and irritating people. For these reasons, young Christians need constant encouragement to stay the course. And there was no one better to provide this kind of encouragement than Barnabas, the great encourager.

Because of the believers' evangelistic fervor and Barnabas's godly influence, the church in Antioch flourished like a field of wildflowers. Soon there was more work than one person could handle, and Barnabas knew he needed help. But who? He had been impressed with Paul when they met in Jerusalem. It had been several years since Barnabas had seen him, but apparently Barnabas had kept up with his whereabouts and knew that Paul was now living in Tarsus.

Sometime in A.D. 43, Barnabas decided to solicit Paul's help, and he headed to Tarsus. This Cilician city was located just around the northeastern corner of the Mediterranean Sea from Antioch, less than one hundred miles west by sea. We don't know what Paul was doing when Barnabas found him in Tarsus. He may have been learning the tentmaking trade that later provided financial support for his missionary journeys. He may have been studying Jewish prophecy and theology and layering them with theology about the coming of Christ. Given Paul's highly active nature, it's likely that he was preaching at every opportunity.

Paul agreed to come back to Antioch with Barnabas, and the two men worked together, leading the burgeoning Jewish-Gentile church and preaching to masses of people. The church continued to grow until it rivaled Jerusalem as a major center of Christianity. It became the frontier outpost of the faith, the strategic launching pad to spread the faith throughout the known world.

It was in Antioch that this movement was officially recognized: "It was at Antioch that the believers were first called Christians" (Acts 11:26). Christianity had gained a solid foothold in the first-century world.

The Offspring Becomes the Parent

One of the gifts the Holy Spirit gave at Pentecost was prophecy. Prophecy involves foretelling events of the future, which is what most people think of when they hear the term. A lesser-known aspect of prophecy is "forth-telling"—bold teaching or exhortation on subjects that are of critical importance to Christians.

Prophets likely circulated among the early churches, delivering messages given to the people through the Holy Spirit. Shortly after Barnabas and Saul began ministering to the church in Antioch, a group of prophets came to them from Jerusalem with a message. When they met with the church, one of them, Agabus, stood up and foretold that a famine would soon devastate the entire Roman world.

The famine arrived in A.D. 45 or 46, during the reign of the Roman emperor Claudius. The worst of it centered in Judea, causing severe suffering and many deaths by starvation. The Jewish historian Josephus confirms the occurrence of this famine in *Antiquities of the*

WHAT ARE FOLLOWERS OF CHRIST CALLED IN THE NEW TESTAMENT?

The New Testament employs ten different words to designate those who have committed to following Christ, and each word describes a facet of what it means to be a Christian. Because we trust Christ, we are *believers*. Because we are born again, we are *sons* (and daughters). Because we follow Christ, we are *disciples*. Because Christ declares us holy, we are *saints*. Because we work for Christ, we are *servants*. Because we love other Christians, we are *brothers and sisters*. Because we have fellowship with Christ, we are *friends*. Because Christ loves us, we are his *beloved*. Because Christ is our future inheritance, we are his *heirs*. But perhaps best of all, because we belong to him and will one day be like him, we are *Christians*.

Jews. He gives an account of a woman named Helena, a convert to Judaism and the queen of a small province of Assyria called Adiabene, who sent massive funds, wheat, and dried figs to Jerusalem to relieve the suffering.[1]

The church in Antioch rallied to send relief to the church in Jerusalem. The members gave sacrificially and sent Barnabas and Saul to Jerusalem to deliver the generous gift.

This was a case of role reversal, much like what many people experience in their families. As parents age and lose their physical health and mental abilities, it often becomes necessary for the child to become the "parent"—the caretaker and provider—exchanging the positions they'd held up to that point. In the relationship between these two churches, Jerusalem was the mother church. It was the birthplace of the church as a whole and the ongoing base for the Jewish church. Antioch was a church plant, an offspring of the church in Jerusalem. It had grown and matured to the point that when the parent church was in need, the offspring church rose to the occasion and provided assistance.

The church in Antioch quickly became a major center of Christianity. It was a natural hub for reaching Asia Minor and Europe, which made it an ideal home base for the apostle Paul, Barnabas, and other missionaries who went on trips to evangelize the Gentile world. In fact, throughout the rest of the book of Acts, the center of activity switches from Jerusalem to Antioch.

The march of the church into all the world had begun.

✦ ✦ ✦

THE CHURCH GAINS A FOOTHOLD

When I consider how quickly the leaders of the Jewish church in Jerusalem accepted the Gentiles as members, I have to admire them. Although they were resistant at first, when Peter recounted the events that led to Cornelius's conversion, they responded with immediate and complete acceptance—and even more amazing, *joy*.

What makes this change of heart so incredible is that the separation from Gentiles had been ingrained into Jews from early in their nation's history. Major changes are never easy—and this seems especially true when it comes to religious changes. When you have followed a lifelong religious practice or belief, thinking it is right and biblical, it is normal to feel automatic resistance if you're told that what you've been doing is not valid.

I've seen it happen. I've known churches to split over even minor changes such as whether to use microphones and electronic screens, whether there should be kitchens in the church building, or what kind of bread to serve for Communion. In each case, the resisting faction felt that the change violated a religious principle and that the innovators had no respect for biblical authority.

The reason we have so many Christian denominations today is

JERUSALEM: THE HOLY CITY

Jerusalem is a significant location for events portrayed throughout the Bible. The city first appears in Genesis 14 as Salem, ruled by the priest-king Melchizedek. It later reverted to paganism until it was conquered by King David's general Joab, when it became the capital of the Jewish nation and the site of the Temple. Nebuchadnezzar destroyed Jerusalem in 586 B.C., and it was rebuilt from 522 to 445 B.C. Several centuries later, Christ's crucifixion, resurrection, and ascension occurred in Jerusalem. In the book of Acts, the Holy Spirit descended on this city, and it became the headquarters of the early church. The Romans destroyed Jerusalem in A.D. 70, but it was rebuilt again. At the end of time, a magnificent New Jerusalem will descend from heaven and usher in Christ's new Kingdom.

because they all differ on what beliefs are crucial to authentic Christianity. Whether the difference involves liturgy, modes of baptism, church organization, or variations in biblical interpretation, the gulf between beliefs is deemed too wide to be bridged.

For the early Jewish church, the exclusion of Gentiles was a long-held tenet. Yet the believers were open to the evidence Peter presented, and they were willing to act on that evidence even though it meant weeding out a belief with deep roots. They said, in essence, "Well, this certainly doesn't fit into our theological box, but it appears that the Lord is doing something new. So we'd better get with this change in the program." When Christians respond in this way, it is evident that the Holy Spirit is at work in their lives. It shows that their desire to please God is stronger than their desire to prove that what they've always believed is written in stone.

The Need for Unity

How can Christians with so many differences merge into a unified whole? The apostle Paul gives the answer in his letter to the church in Rome. They were having trouble reconciling some of the long-standing beliefs held by both Jews and formerly pagan Gentiles. Both groups came into the church carrying baggage from their previous beliefs, mostly involving dietary laws and the observance of ritual holidays. Some Jews were reluctant to eat meat from Rome's marketplace because it might have been sacrificed to pagan idols. Some vegetarians believed it was wrong to eat meat of any kind. Some believers felt that they should continue to observe certain ritual holidays from their previous religions. Christians from each group tended to judge one another, and their differences threatened the unity of the church.

Paul knew that these differences were not central to the faith. Christians who were strong in their walk with Christ could freely eat or not eat meat and observe or not observe non-idolatrous holidays without affecting their faith. But Christians whose faith didn't go as deep felt a need to prop themselves up with these beliefs they'd carried all their lives. Here was Paul's message to them:

> Accept other believers who are weak in faith, and don't argue with them about what they think is right or wrong. For instance, one person believes it's all right to eat anything. But another believer with a sensitive conscience will eat only vegetables. Those who feel free to eat anything must not look down on those who don't. And those who don't eat certain foods must not condemn those who do, for God has accepted them. Who are you to condemn someone else's servants? Their own master will judge whether they stand or fall. And with the Lord's help, they will stand and receive his approval.
>
> In the same way, some think one day is more holy than another day, while others think every day is alike. You should each be fully convinced that whichever day you choose is acceptable. Those who worship the Lord on a special day do it to honor him. Those who eat any kind of food do so to honor the Lord, since they give thanks to God before eating. And those who refuse to eat certain foods also want to please the Lord and give thanks to God.   ROMANS 14:1-6

It's true that there are some conflicts among Christians that are too wide to bridge. Differences that violate the central beliefs of the faith, such as those articulated in the Apostles' Creed, cannot be accepted without gutting the core of Christianity. But Paul is saying that many of our differences don't really matter to God, and we shouldn't make them tests of authentic Christianity.

Our peripheral variations in belief should never be obstacles to fellowship. Jesus himself prayed that all who believed in him would be unified: "I am praying not only for these disciples but also for all who will ever believe in me through their message. I pray that they will all be one, just as you and I are one—as you are in me, Father, and I am in you. And may they be in us so that the world will believe you sent me" (John 17:20-21).

This unity that Christ prayed for has not yet occurred. There are more than two hundred Christian denominations in the United States,[2] and it seems impossible to bring unity from such widespread division. But as we can see from the events in Acts 11, this task of unifying widely divergent groups is not impossible with God.

It may well be that God will bring about unity among American believers in the not-too-distant future. Repression of Christian practices is increasing in Western countries, as evidenced by restrictions on religious speech, the banning of prayer and Bible reading in public venues, enforced tolerance of immorality, and the denial of conscience rights in various professions. History tells us that these trends are likely to accelerate to the point that in order for believers to practice authentic Christianity, churches must disband and go underground. This would mean that faithful and determined Christians from many denominations would likely meet together in small groups in homes, warehouses, or other available facilities. The mix of denominational beliefs in these groups would certainly be eclectic, but in such a situation, those peripheral beliefs would no longer stand in the way. The core beliefs of Christianity would become central and essential.

When these things come to pass, Christians will do well to look at Acts 11 and follow the lead of the churches in Jerusalem and Antioch. They will find freedom in foregoing their previous denominational differences and focusing on their common identity as Christians.

The Gift of Humility

When Barnabas realized that the church in Antioch was becoming too large for him to manage, the first person he thought of to help him was Saul. Barnabas had seen the brilliance, talent, and potential greatness of Saul, and he figured he could find no better colleague.

The unique thing about this choice is that Barnabas must have known that Saul would likely eclipse him. Barnabas had earned a position of high respect in the church. He had been a major influence among the believers in Jerusalem and had been sent to Antioch as just the man to handle the diversity of the church. With Saul back in the picture, Barnabas would almost certainly play second fiddle—the number-two man serving under a newcomer with a checkered past.

But Barnabas cared nothing about power or prestige; he was willing to give all that up for the greater good. His sole interest was the expansion of God's Kingdom. And if Saul was the man who could make it happen, then Barnabus would be his biggest fan. Like John the Baptist, Barnabas was willing to decrease while Saul increased if it meant advancement of the cause of Christ (John 3:25-30, NKJV).

Barnabas's willingness to choose Saul was an act of humility—the kind we seldom see today. But it was exactly the kind of attitude and behavior that should characterize every Christian. If Christians, especially church leaders, consistently cared about the well-being of the church more than their own prestige, my guess is that 95 percent of church problems would vanish.

The Rivalry That Never Happened

The church in Antioch flourished so much under Barnabas and Saul that it soon began to overshadow its mother church in Jerusalem. The two churches could well have become rivals. The believers in Jerusalem in particular, being in the birthplace of Christianity and its first center, could have felt threatened by this upstart half-Gentile church in pagan territory. They could have assumed this church plant was trying to pull off a coup of sorts—something like a corporate takeover. The believers in Antioch, on the other hand, could have let their success go to their heads. They could have seen the Christians in Jerusalem as a bunch of stodgy has-beens and left them behind.

But neither of these attitudes developed. It seems that the same kind of humility demonstrated by Barnabas was prevalent within these two churches. These believers were not competitors; they were cooperators. The overarching interest of both groups was to advance the cause of Christ.

This spirit of serving with love, cooperation, and mutual respect was evident during the famine predicted by Agabus. The church in Antioch sacrificed to send relief to the hard-hit church in Jerusalem. Instead of rivalry or pride, these Christians were marked by the kind of unity that comes from the Holy Spirit.

Meeting the Need of All Humanity

Why was there such an explosion of conversions in Antioch? One answer may be its location. Stationed on trade routes by land and by river, it was one of the three major cities in the Roman Empire. It was only fifteen miles from a Mediterranean harbor, giving it further access to trade and travel.

Because Antioch was such a booming trade center, travelers from many countries flowed in and out of the city. Most were pagans. The fact that they were pagans, however, did not mean they weren't religious. Most believed at some level in the existence of supreme beings, and some were devout in their beliefs. Many worshiped Greek and Roman gods. Others were skeptical about the validity of these gods but knew there must be a supernatural power of some kind. They sensed that there was a rift between themselves and the gods, so they offered sacrifices at the countless temples and altars strewn throughout the empire.

All throughout history, people have sensed that there's a higher power. Primitive people feared thunder, lightning, hailstorms, earthquakes, eclipses, or volcanic eruptions, viewing them as expressions of an angry deity. And throughout history, people have felt out of sync with this higher power and have offered sacrifices of various kinds as attempts at appeasement. In short, humans have always recognized that something is wrong between people and God and have searched for ways to become right with him.

While the ancient myths about the gods were terribly misguided, they were not altogether devoid of truth. According to the famous novelist J. R. R. Tolkien, these were merely attempts to articulate a reality that people sensed. The myths about dying gods and human sacrifices were dim and distorted pictures that prefigured the truth revealed in Christ.

This cultural backdrop made Antioch ideally situated to reveal the truth to pagans in the first-century world. They were already religious by nature. They sensed their alienation from a deity and their need to make things right. Since Antioch was a major crossroads for these pagans, many saw the truth they'd been longing for as it played out in the lives of the new believers there. They had been prepared by their own religious yearnings, and now Christianity offered exactly what they had been looking for.

Antioch was also ideally positioned to launch the gospel into Asia Minor, Europe, and cities bordering the Mediterranean Sea. With the masses of travelers coming in and out of the city, those who entered enlarged the already growing church. Those who left carried the message of the Good News to foreign ports and cities. Antioch was the place where the answer to the universal need of humankind was launched into the wider world.

By the providence of God, this city headquartered an active church headed by Christians who maintained their vision and diligence. Their evangelistic fervor never slackened. Charles Swindoll tells a personal story that illustrates why this church was so dynamic.

I have played enough sports, been in touch with enough coaches, watched enough games, and read closely enough to know that there's one strategy that's deadly. And it's so subtle. You think you can win by doing it, but you lose. It's called sitting on the lead. . . .

When I was in high school, our basketball team went to state finals in Texas. In one state final game we were ahead at halftime 26 to 18. The coach said, "Now we got 'em. We got 'em. Just take it easy." You know what? We lost, 41 to 40. Why? Because we tried to sit on our lead. We thought we had them beat, so we played with a maintenance mentality.

A growing church never gets so far ahead that it can afford to "sit on the lead." Complacency is a major peril to evangelism.[3]

Their Need Is Our Need

In our modern, sophisticated culture, we are no different from the people in these pagan societies. We have exactly the same need they had. As fallen humans, we share with them in sensing our alienation from God, and we desperately need a way to be reconciled to him.

It seems, however, that many people today don't sense this need for reconciliation as acutely as people from previous eras did. Our ease and affluence dull our awareness of just how needy we are. But this need to become right with God is real, and it is imperative that we keep this truth before us at all times. We carry the infection of sin in our lives, and we bear guilt for those sins. We cannot be reconciled to God until that guilt is removed, and it can be removed only through the sacrifice of Christ.

Christ is the only way to be reconciled with God. Only he can remove the guilt of sin and make us pure in God's sight. He is the one and only way to eternal life.

AFTERWORD

The book of Acts chronicles many beginnings—the beginning of the church and the beginning of the A.D. era, as well as the launching of the gospel into all the world.

These first eleven chapters of Acts tell the story of how our redemption from sin began at the Cross, spread beyond the Jews, and began its relentless march to bless all nations of the world. It's the story of how the gospel was taken to the three major groups Jesus identified in his great commission: the Jews, the Samaritans, and the Gentiles.

This book ends the first phase of the book of Acts. It marks the completion of the start of the church. From this point forward, the emphasis of Acts changes. After a brief interlude in chapter 12, it becomes primarily the story of the apostle Paul's missionary travels throughout Asia Minor and parts of Europe.

Although our journey ends here for now, I encourage you to keep reading the book of Acts. It is one of the most gripping narratives in the Bible, filled with action, suspense, and danger. It is also a biographical portrait of the most dedicated Christian you're ever likely to find. Paul's career inspires us and models for us what a Christian should be in this world.

As you continue following the steps of Jesus and the apostles and the believers in the early church, I pray that you will be inspired to emulate their submission and dedication. After all, their story is our story too.

NOTES

THE DAY GOD DIED
1. James Stalker, *The Life of Christ* (Grand Rapids, MI: Zondervan, 1983), 122.

FROM GRIEF TO GLORY
1. Carl Sagan, *Billions and Billions: Thoughts on Life and Death at the Brink of the Millennium* (New York: Random House Publishing Group, 1997), 258.
2. John Stott, *Christ in Conflict* (Downers Grove, IL: InterVarsity Press, 2013), 56.
3. Frank Morison, *Who Moved the Stone?* (Grand Rapids, MI: Zondervan, 2002).
4. Charles Colson and Harold Fickett, *The Faith: What Christians Believe, Why They Believe It, and Why It Matters* (Grand Rapids, MI: Zondervan, 2008), 93.
5. Adapted from Josh McDowell and Sean McDowell, *Evidence for the Resurrection* (Ventura, CA: Regal, 2009).
6. Ibid., 308.
7. Daniel Fuller, *Easter Faith and History* (Grand Rapids, MI: Eerdmans, 1965), 259.
8. McDowell and McDowell, *Evidence for the Resurrection*, 309.
9. J. P. Moreland, quoted in Lee Strobel, *The Case for Christ: A Journalist's Personal Investigation of the Evidence for Jesus* (Grand Rapids, MI: Zondervan, 1998), 385.

WIND AND FIRE
1. C. S. Lewis, *Mere Christianity* (New York: The Macmillan Co., 1952), 36.
2. James Montgomery Boice, *Acts: An Expositional Commentary* (Grand Rapids, MI: Baker Books, 1997), 56.
3. R. Kent Hughes, *Romans: Righteousness from Heaven* (Wheaton, IL: Crossway Books, 1991), 284.
4. Max Lucado, *Outlive Your Life* (Nashville, TN: Thomas Nelson, 2010), 54–57.
5. J. C. Macaulay, *Expository Commentary on Acts* (Chicago: Moody Press, 1978), 39.

6. John R. W. Stott, *The Message of Acts* (Downers Grove, IL: InterVarsity Press, 1990), 87.

OPPORTUNITY AND OPPOSITION

1. Quoted in Lloyd Albert Johnson, *A Toolbox for Humanity* (Victoria: Trafford Publishing, 2006), 23.
2. Quoted in Jessica Durando, "15 of Nelson Mandela's Best Quotes," *USA Today*, December 6, 2013, http://www.usatoday.com/story/news/nation-now/2013/12/05 /nelson-mandela-quotes/3775255/.
3. C. S. Lewis, *The Screwtape Letters* (New York: HarperCollins, 1996), 161.
4. James A. Brooks, *The New American Commentary: Mark* (Nashville: Broadman Press, 1991), 193.
5. Ibid., 193.
6. Mark Buchanan in *Glimpses of Heaven: Surprising Stories of Hope and Encouragement* (Eugene, OR: Harvest House, 2013), 70.

HYPOCRITES AND HEROES

1. John Phillips, *Exploring Acts* (Grand Rapids, MI: Kregel Publications, 1986), 94.
2. Ibid., 94.
3. Colin Smith, "God Will Bring Justice for You," *PreachingToday.com*, http://www .preachingtoday.com/sermons/outlines/2012/february/godbringjustice.html.
4. Michael Card, "Wounded in the House of Friends," *Virtue*, March/April 1991, 28–29, 69.
5. John Piper, *Let the Nations Be Glad!* (Grand Rapids, MI: Baker Academic, 2010), 113–14.

THE DEATH OF A SERVANT

1. Story adapted from Pat Williams, *The Paradox of Power: A Transforming View of Leadership* (New York: Warner Books, 2002), 199.
2. Gary Inrig, *A Call to Excellence* (Wheaton, IL: Victor Books, 1985), 98.
3. Martin Luther King Jr., quoted in David E. Garland, *The NIV Application Commentary: Mark* (Grand Rapids, MI: Zondervan, 2011), Kindle edition.
4. Calvin Miller, *Into the Depths of God* (Ada, MI: Bethany House, 2000), 150.
5. Quoted in Craig Brian Larson, *Perfect Illustrations for Every Topic and Occasion* (Carol Stream, IL: Tyndale House, 2002), 181–82.

THE TRAVELING PREACHER

1. Tim Keller, "Preaching Hell in a Tolerant Age," *Christianity Today*, Fall 1997, http://www.christianitytoday.com/le/1997/fall/7l4042.html.
2. See the Apostles' Creed and the Nicene Creed.
3. C. S. Lewis, "The Efficacy of Prayer," in *The World's Last Night and Other Essays* (New York: Harcourt, Brace & World, 1960), 3.

THE MAN WHO SAW THE LIGHT

1. George Lyttleton, *Observations on the Conversion and Apostleship of St. Paul* (London: The Religious Tract Society, 1868), 75.

2. C. S. Lewis, *Surprised by Joy* (New York: Harcourt, Brace & Company, 1955), 224, 228–29.

3. John MacArthur, *The MacArthur New Testament Commentary: Acts 1–12* (Chicago: Moody Press, 1994), 270.

4. Dan Graves, "Alcoholic Mel Trotter Delivered from Drink," *Christianity.com*, http://www.christianity.com/church/church-history/timeline/1801-1900/alcoholic-mel-trotter-delivered-from-drink-11630650.html.

STORMY BEGINNINGS

1. J. Oswald Sanders, *Bible Men of Faith* (Chicago: Moody, 1970), 202.

2. Tim Kimmel, quoted in Alice Gray, *Stories for the Heart* (Sisters, OR: Multnomah, 2001), 59–60.

THE LIFE GOD BLESSES

1. C. S. Lewis, *The Horse and His Boy* (New York: Macmillan, 1954), 122–23.

2. "Little Is Much When God Is in It," words and music by Kittie L. Suffield, 1924.

A WALL COMES DOWN

1. Lewis, "The Efficacy of Prayer," 9.

2. *Bits and Pieces*, November 1989, 24.

INTO ALL THE WORLD

1. Flavius Josephus, *Josephus: Complete Works* (Grand Rapids, MI: Kregel Publications, 1963), 416.

2. Statistic drawn from Samuel S. Hill and Frank S. Mead, *Handbook of Denominations in the United States* (Nashville: Abingdon Press, 1994), http://mesacc.edu/~thoqh49081/handouts/denominations.html.

3. Charles R. Swindoll, *The Tale of the Tardy Oxcart* (Nashville: Word Publishing, 1998), 184.

ABOUT THE AUTHOR

Dr. David Jeremiah serves as senior pastor of Shadow Mountain Community Church in El Cajon, California. He is the founder and host of Turning Point, a ministry committed to providing Christians with sound Bible teaching relevant to today's changing times through radio, television, the Internet, live events, and resource materials and books. A bestselling author, Dr. Jeremiah has written more than forty books, including *Captured by Grace, Living with Confidence in a Chaotic World, What in the World Is Going On?, The Coming Economic Armageddon, God Loves You: He Always Has—He Always Will, What Are You Afraid Of?,* and *Agents of the Apocalypse.*

Dr. Jeremiah's commitment to teaching the complete Word of God continues to make him a sought-after speaker and writer. His passion for reaching the lost and encouraging believers in their faith is demonstrated through his faithful communication of biblical truths.

A dedicated family man, Dr. Jeremiah and his wife, Donna, have four grown children and twelve grandchildren.

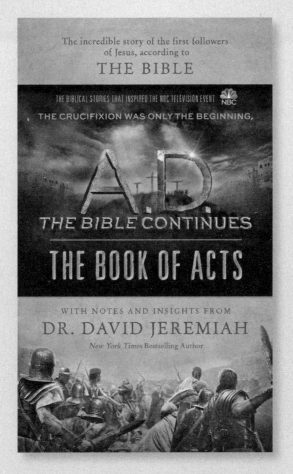